EP Sport Backpacking

○ Denotes titles currently
available in paperback as well
as hardback

EP PUBLISHING LIMITED

EP SPORT Backpacking

Don Robinson

ISBN 0 7158 0601 7 (cased)
ISBN 0 7158 0652 1 (limp)

Published by EP Publishing Ltd, East Ardsley,
Wakefield, West Yorkshire, 1981

Reprinted 1982

Text Photoset in 11/13pt Times by G. Beard &
Son Ltd., Brighton, Sussex

Printed and bound in Great Britain by
McCorquodale (Scotland) Ltd., Glasgow

Acknowledgements

I should like to thank in particular Dr W. K. Griffiths of the Physics
Department, University of Leeds, for his work in evaluating the
efficiency of backpacking stoves and, more importantly, for his
continued support and encouragement whilst writing this book.

I am indebted to Dr J. H. Keighley and Mr Martin Penny of the
Outdoor Equipment and Pursuits Section, Department of Textile
Industries, University of Leeds, for their considerable help with the
Appendix on Fibres and Fabrics, and also to Miss Pat Taylor, for her
help with the chapter on Food and catering.

I should also like to thank my many friends and colleagues, too
numerous to mention by name, for their help and assistance in
creating this book, especially those who co-operated in the
production of the pictures.

Warning

There are frequent references in the text to the use of polythene and
polythene bags. Always use thick heavy-gauge polythene, which you can get
from a builder's merchant, or one of the survival bags sold in most outdoor
shops. Under *no* circumstances must you use thin-gauge polythene which
may cling to your face and suffocate you.

Contents

Preface

This book is about an ever-growing and popular activity, 'backpacking'. This word may not be familiar to everybody, but is far more apt than the euphemistic expression 'lightweight camping'. Perhaps it should have been entitled 'Bivouacking to backpacking in easy stages'. It is based on a progression from elementary sleeping out in the open in summer using simple inexpensive gear to the most sophisticated and expensive equipment for winter backpacking. The book is aimed at beginner and expert alike. It covers the fundamentals of living in the great outdoors – food, shelter and clothing linked to the most basic form of transport: one's own feet. At the same time it emphasises the need to respect and protect the ecology and the delicate eco-systems of the woods, moors and mountains in which the 'backpacker' lives and travels.

There is no substitute for knowledge, experience, planning and a proper respect for nature.

'Yours to enjoy, not to destroy'

1 The new ethic-minimum environmental impact

As urban development increases year by year, growing like a cancer across the surface of the earth, the available countryside and open spaces decrease annually. Pollution in all its forms further threatens what remains of the unspoilt scenery. Man himself is solely responsible for this damage. Each year increasing numbers of car-borne people visit the countryside, adding to the problem. Fortunately 80 per cent of these tourists do not move far from their cars and it is not difficult for those who want to find peace and solitude only a few miles from the 'honey-pot areas'.

However, walking and camping are becoming more popular, possibly as an antidote to the pressures of modern society. More young people are being introduced to adventurous outdoor activities than ever before by schools, youth organisations and the mass media. Even writing this book is likely to further increase the numbers visiting the remoter countryside. One might ask, why produce another book on backpacking? The important point is that there is still plenty of room for everyone provided that they respect and understand the ecology. All campers, hikers, climbers, canoeists and users of the natural environment need to adopt a more positive approach to protecting the very important resources they seek to enjoy. It is vital that it is protected and enhanced for future generations. Not to do so is selfish. Preservation does not mean sterilisation, but educated and sympathetic usage. How then does this affect the backpacker?

First, he must grasp the notion of *Minimum Impact on the Environment*. This means rather more than the still very valid old adage: 'Take nothing but photographs, leave nothing but footprints'. Ideally it would be best not to leave the footprints. Every action taken, every piece of behaviour should be considered in the light of what would happen if say eight million people did it (this is about the number of annual visitors to some of our National Parks). Whilst it may seem harmless to drop the odd toffee paper or bury the odd can or plastic wrapper, if this were multiplied by eight million then clearly it would be unacceptable. So it's wrong to leave anything, no matter how small, in the countryside. Some wrappers and other items are bio-degradable but many ecologists would question the acceptability of leaving even these items behind. Every year there are more and more hikers, walkers and campers which means there is a long-term cumulative effect. In fifty years' time the quantity of buried plastic and rubbish in the natural environment will be intolerable unless from this moment onwards everyone has a positive attitude to taking their litter home. The American backpackers' slogan 'Pack it in, pack it out' is unquestionably the right approach.

Another aspect of minimum impact is that which is caused by too many people going to the same popular places or following the same popular routes. Currently there is a lot of debate about long-distance footpaths and the advantages and disadvantages of creating more of these. The main drawback is that very soon the tens of thousands of feet following these waymarked routes simply trample down and wear off the surface vegetation. The wind and rain soon remove the soil or in areas of poor drainage create a quagmire. Either way we get permanent, irreparable damage to the landscape. This is already evident on sections of the popular Pennine Way, where in places plastic mesh had to be used to reinforce the path, and on routes such

Plastic mesh reinforces the path along the Pennine Way

Peat 'groughs' on the Derbyshire moors

Strenuous walking over soft ground

as the Three Peaks of Yorkshire and the Lyke Wake Walk on the North Yorkshire moors.

The answer is to encourage enterprise and more imaginative route planning so that the wear and tear is more evenly distributed. Normally the good backpacker associates his activity with remote places, solitude and wilderness areas. However, completing one of the recognised long-distance footpaths such as the 270-mile long Pennine Way does have a great appeal to many people and this form of backpacking should not be decried. Backpacking is all about doing your own thing with your own food and shelter on your back, not interfering with or upsetting other people or the ecology, simply moving through the landscape unobtrusively – like a ship at sea in the night.

This brings us to the growing current move towards minimum *visual* impact. Up to now there has been a considerable campaign to persuade mountaineers and hill walkers to wear safety colours, e.g. orange, red or yellow coloured anoraks and overtrousers, red socks and coloured woolly hats. Of course this has a great deal of merit if one is responsible for young people in a wild environment, since it makes them easier to locate and rescue. Rescue personnel also support the wearing of bright safety colours, for it often makes their job much less difficult. However, now that we have thousands of people walking in the countryside every weekend the mass of coloured specks moving about the landscape is becoming visually offensive. The same applies to bright orange tents. One or two in the view may be acceptable, one or two hundred are not. What is the solution?

The answer has to be a personal one, based on the individual situation. Solitary walkers and groups of young novices might be well advised to wear safety colours, for they are much more at risk than, say, a small group of experienced people. The latter could quite well wear clothing in natural brown or green colours, since the risk to them is minimal and it would be an appropriate sign of their skill and experience. In many cases it is practical to adopt a compromise solution: summer and fine weather clothing in natural colours, winter and bad weather clothing in bright safety colours. Solitary walkers should consider always wearing at least one brightly coloured article which can be seen from a distance. Anyone who has spent days

Minimum impact clothing for the countryside

of his life searching for missing hikers who are dressed in all tweed clothing in the middle of a moor of deep heather will tell you why; often the remains of such people are not found until months later. Finally, it is sensible to consider the variables of time of year, country to be covered and so on before making a choice of colour (see Chapter 6). Remember there is a world of difference between walking through low level agricultural country in summer (safety colours unnecessary and undesirable – could be dangerous if there were a bull about) and backpacking in the Scottish highlands in winter.

All those who use the natural environment for their recreation and enjoyment have a duty to consider the wider issues as well. In modern times it is not sufficient just to do your own thing properly. Practising the 'minimum impact' code is good, taking home rubbish left by other people as well is better, but these things alone are not enough to protect and preserve our natural heritage. They will not stop the march of so-called technological progress and the inexorable increase in visitor pressures on the countryside. You might consider becoming a 'Friend of the Earth' (address on p. 115) to support the long-term protection of the environment in all its forms. In America, for example, they have persuaded some states to forbid by law the sale of non-returnable containers. In other words every can and bottle carries a significant deposit. If this happened in Britain it would have a dramatic effect on the thousands of tins and bottles currently being left on our hill and mountain tops. Recycling this kind of container would also help to preserve the finite resources of 'Planet Earth'. (It's the only one we've got.) If you enjoy the great outdoors you have an obligation to lend your support to ideas and schemes of this kind.

Studying a sastrugi – safety colours for remote area in winter

2 How to begin

A forest trail. Be especially careful not to start a fire: 'one tree can make 50,000 matches – one match can burn down 50,000 trees'

'A journey of a thousand miles starts with a single step'

Day excursions on foot

The essence of learning and gaining experience, especially on one's own, is to progress in easy stages from the known into the unknown. Experience is the best teacher and progressing carefully in small steps is the safest way to gain experience. Do not try to run before you can walk.

Nearly everyone has some previous knowledge of the countryside, no matter how small. This then must be the starting point. First consider doing some simple day hikes in low-level countryside. Concentrate on the rudiments of travel using whatever equipment and clothing you may possess. An essential item, of course, is a map of the area you intend to visit. In many parts of the country booklets giving local walks and rambles are available. Initially these will help you to get some ideas of where to go and points of interest to look out for en route. However, an Ordnance Survey map soon becomes a must. Whenever possible buy the new 1:25000 (2½ inches to 1 mile, 4 centimetres to 1 kilometre) scale maps. These are ideal for walkers and illustrate a wealth of detailed information. You can almost see yourself travelling across the map. They show roads, paths, walls, streams, buildings, woods, water and a lot of other information such as camp sites, good view points and mountain rescue posts. The more popular areas are covered by Outdoor Leisure Maps. If these are not available then you will find that the Ordnance Survey maps 1:50000 scale (1¼ inches to 1 mile, 2 centimetres to 1 kilometre) are adequate but they do not contain quite as much detail. A catalogue giving information on all maps published by the Ordnance Survey is available free of charge from the Ordnance Survey headquarters (address on p. 115).

When planning your initial walks err on the modest side. Do not be

11

too ambitious. It all depends on what you are used to (your level of fitness) and other variables such as steepness of ground, footwear and weather conditions. Five miles is a long way to some people whereas twenty-five miles is considered by others to be just a stroll.

Study the map and plan a route which keeps you off the roads as much as possible, but you *must* stick to public Rights of Way. These are normally shown on the O.S. maps as a fine line made up of green dots. At the side of every map is a description of the meaning of all the signs, colours and symbols used on the map. Study these before starting out. In easy low-lying country in the summer time a compass is not really necessary, but care must be taken to follow one's progress on the map at all times. The art of finding one's way is never to get lost: you should always know exactly where you are on your map. It is a good idea to forecast by 'reading' the map what you should see in the next ten minutes or half a mile. For example, you might be able to forecast that in a quarter of a mile you will cross a stream running from right to left, followed closely by a barn on your right, soon to be followed by a small wood below the path. This gives good practice in interpreting maps, is more interesting and you will soon discover if you have gone wrong. Once you have lost your way it can be quite difficult deciding exactly where you are on the map.

If you decide to buy a compass early on then buy the best you can afford. A sound purchase will last you many years and will help you

Learn to cook a simple meal to begin
with, first in summer . . .

. . . then in winter. Note the sheltered position of the stove

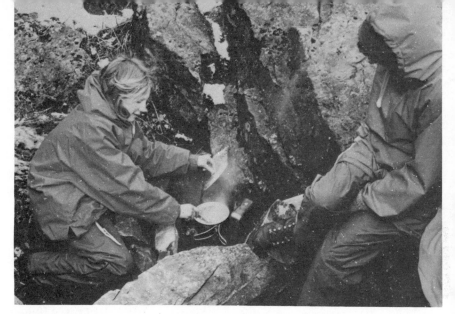

navigate in the most difficult mountain terrain later on, once you have learnt how to use it. Small circular compasses with undamped needles are almost useless. Aim to purchase a liquid-filled Silva-type compass (see p. 38). They are accurate and easy to use, and a leaflet of instructions is sold with the compass. Practise using it as soon as possible.

Initially it is a good idea to take a Thermos flask containing a hot drink together with some sandwiches or similar food on your day's walk. Normally it is better to eat a little and often rather than one large meal. Always have some snacks such as chocolate ready in a handy pocket so that you can eat a little whilst moving. Walking burns up quite a lot of energy (calories) so you don't have to worry too much about your weight (see p. 84).

When you have done a few walks and are getting the hang of things you can start learning how to cook yourself a meal out in the open. Instead of taking a packed lunch, buy a stove (see Chapter 5), learn how to use it at home in the garden and then cook your lunch on it during your walking day. Just a simple meal to begin with. Make yourself a hot drink or some soup, cook a few beans, bacon or sausage. The idea is to get used to cooking out in the open in all weather. Providing yourself with hot nourishing food in any climatic

'Poly bags kill me'

Respect countryside life

conditions is an absolute must for the serious backpacker. In winter camping your life might depend on it. To begin with try to choose a calm dry day in the summer time. Then perhaps on a wet windy day and much later in cold, wet, generally bad conditions. Look upon it as a challenge to be able to make a simple meal in any circumstances. It needs practice.

Whatever stove you choose (see Chapter 5) you will need to get it out of the wind. It must be sheltered, otherwise you may not be able to light it and it certainly will not work very well because the wind will blow the heat away to the side – away from your cooking pot. Try to find a hollow, a wall or some natural windbreak. If this is not possible make a windbreak using stones, a rucksack or even your own body. Some people carry a portable windbreak, consisting of three rods 12 inches (30cm) long and a short length of fabric. The Optimus and the Trangia meths stoves are possible exceptions to this; in both, the cooking pot and burner form an integrated unit and they sometimes work better in a moderate breeze. The heat from any stove will kill the grass and vegetation beneath it. It is not usually noticeable at the time but if you return a few days later you will see an ugly brown patch instead of green grass. So either stand your stove on bare ground or rocks or in some way make a heat barrier between the stove and the plants. A flat stone, wood or even woollen mittens will do. Always put the stones back where they came from. Remember not to leave any signs of your passing.

Finally, be aware of the Country Code:
- ☐ Stay on the footpath or the line of the Right of Way if no visible path exists
- ☐ Close and fasten gates behind you
- ☐ Avoid causing any damage
- ☐ Keep dogs under control
- ☐ Take your litter home – plus some!
- ☐ Guard against risk of fire
- ☐ Safeguard water supplies from pollution
- ☐ Protect wild life, plants and trees
- ☐ Respect the countryside life

Perhaps at this point you might like to consider starting a log or record book. Usually an inexpensive note book is adequate. Many people like to keep such a record and a great many others wish they

Date	Route	Weather	Companions	Notes
9.9.80	Three Peaks	Fair	John Brown Tim Smith	Saw three Lapwings nests.
				Took 8½ hrs.

had started one at the beginning of their walking career. All you need to do is rule some columns down the pages to note the date, route, weather conditions, names of companions, and anything else which interests you such as wild flowers, birds, animals, historic places etc. The notes are usually a reflection of your personal interests and hobbies. At the end of each month or year it is interesting to see what you have accomplished. Unless you are a budding author it is best to keep your note book brief and simple. Otherwise it becomes too time-consuming and will quickly fall into disuse.

As soon as you can, consider also obtaining a camera. Just a modest instamatic camera will do for a start. It will help you record and capture some of these good times and places which you are bound to discover. The photos help to keep memories alive and are good to show to your friends.

Summer bivouacking
'Bivouacking' is spending the night out in the open without a tent, normally sleeping in an improvised or temporary shelter. You may ask why is there a section on bivouacking in a book essentially about backpacking. The answer is simple and twofold. It has a lot to do with cost (money) and experience (survival).

To equip oneself completely with good-quality backpacking equipment such as boots, warm clothes, waterproofs, rucksack, tent, stove, sleeping bag etc. will cost you around £300 at current (1981) prices, and not many people have that sort of money available at one time. Personally I don't believe you have to wait until you can afford everything before making a start. A middle-aged backpacker recently said to me: 'People who can't afford to buy proper equipment shouldn't be doing it'. But many of us learnt to live and travel in the wilderness areas with little money and before plastics such as nylon and polythene were invented, and there is no reason why young people to-day should not do the same. Naturally bivouacking has some limitations, but it also has many advantages as well as a financial one.

Firstly it is a basic survival technique. Anyone who knows how to bivouac in all sorts of different environments, wild moorlands and desolate snow fields, is infinitely safer than someone who does not. Modern tents are designed to withstand pretty bad weather. But no

Tents burn down ...   ... and blow away!

tent is infallible. Sooner or later they blow down or tear and occasionally burn down. The loss of one's tent in a remote area in a winter storm could be fatal unless one knew how to make a bivouac – not only *knew* how but have *practised* the art. In a harsh environment such as a storm or a blizzard in the hills the shelter takes priority over food. Victims of hypothermia (exposure to cold), or deep body cooling, are likely to die unless given adequate protection in a shelter where rest, warmth and other remedial measures can be given (see Chapter 9). It might be a good idea if tents were used as a reward for having mastered the art of bivouacking.

Having done several day walks and learnt something about walking, map reading and cooking, the next step in the progression is to embark on a two-day journey with an overnight stop. Obviously you will need some extra equipment. The main items would be a sleeping bag and a large sheet of builders' polythene: a sheet 8ft (2.5m) square would be adequate for one person; a piece 8 x 12ft (2.5 x 3.5m) is good for two or three people (the rolls are often 12ft (3.5m) wide). A small piece is required to lie on as a ground sheet. This polythene is relatively cheap (£1) compared to a tent (£70-£100). In addition, a foamed closed cell polythene mat such as a Karrimat or a foam-filled self-inflating mattress such as 'Calipak' would greatly

Bivouacs using rocks or existing walls

a A first attempt at bivouacking, using a broken-down wall in a farmer's field, *with* the farmer's permission

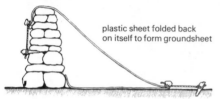

plastic sheet folded back on itself to form groundsheet

b Another form of shelter against a wall. Thread the cord through the wall or tie it to a jutting-out stone in the wall

c A shelter between two boulders

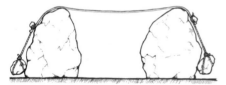

rain

d In wet weather rain runs down the rock and into the 'bivvy' unless you take the poly sheet over the top of the boulder before anchoring it

e Summer shelter against overhanging boulder side, sealing off with a wall of stones

add to your comfort at night. It also means you can use a cheaper sleeping bag (see p. 51) because of the improved ground insulation. Your rucksack, which you may have been borrowing up to now, might not be large enough to hold this new set of equipment. There is a bewildering range of rucksacks on the market and you should study the information in Chapter 5 before making a purchase.

Your first attempts at sleeping out in a 'bivvy' must be done in the summer time in a safe place. Not *too* far from habitation and at a fairly low level, just in case things don't go too well. Rough country or woods are best where some natural building materials are available and where preferably you can get out of sight of other people. However, every inch of this country belongs to someone and you *must* seek permission before sleeping out on someone else's land. Remember *Minimum Impact*. Use green or dark polythene if you can get it. Do not damage trees in any way. Do not remove stones from walls. Replace or redistribute any stones that you use. Make sure you leave no trace of your having been there.

You should allow at least two hours, maybe longer at first, to build

A simple dome shelter made of plastic, using a pack-frame as a support, located in an old quarry

Variations of tree supports for bivouacs

a Cone-type all-weather bivouac hung from a single support over a tree branch, with the edges weighted with stones. Use the anchorage method shown on p. 21

b Tent-style 'bivvy' made from a large polythene tube, slung between two trees and pegged down at corners This type of shelter can also be made with a single sheet of polythene (see p. 19)

your shelter. Therefore arrive at your chosen site in good time. Bivouacking is something of an art and can only be learnt by doing it. There are no hard and fast rules except that it should be weatherproof and as comfortable as possible. Living rough and dirty like a pig and suffering a lot of discomfort is a sign that you are not coping with this new situation. With a little practice you should be able to live comfortably and hygienically in a bivouac, even in bad weather, and enjoy good well-presented meals. You may have a few mild disasters to begin with but you will soon learn – experience *is* the best teacher.

On arrival at your destination, have a good look round for 'natural shelters' such as a large boulder overhanging on one side. Maybe there will be two or more boulders together that could be utilised. In woods there are often trees and boughs that have potential for shelter (guard against fire – if it's very dry do not use a wood). Peat moors and stony areas on hills, even old quarries, make potential 'bivvy' sites.

As well as your 'poly sheet' you will need a plentiful supply of string and something to cut it with. A plastic sheet has an infinite number of anchorage points on it if you use the method shown in the illustration on p. 21. Eyeletted sheets often dictate and influence the 'bivvy' design, whereas those without eyelets give endless scope for imaginative ideas. (Some basic construction details are shown on p. 21.)

d Alternative method of tree support: use an 'up and over' loop and one of the anchorages shown on p. 21

c This is the same type of shelter as shown on the bottom of p.18 but made with a single sheet of polythene (so it does not incorporate a ground sheet). It is not very suitable for windy conditions, so choose a sheltered place

The ideal bivouac house should have a fairly level floor area, well drained and one that will not collect water in heavy rain. Study the lie of the land; try to visualise which way the surface water will run in a thunderstorm. Next make sure that you have sufficient head room at one end, maybe 3 or 4ft (1-1.3m) high. This will probably take care of the next point, which is to make sure your plastic roof has some kind of gradient and will not collect water. Sometimes it is necessary to arrange a centre pole with a stick or pack frame. Make sure that the 'poly sheet' is well anchored down. Strong winds can play havoc with plastic. Make it as draught-proof as you can by stuffing dead grass or bracken between the stones, but allow some ventilation to cut down condensation on the inside of your roof. Face the doorway away from the wind and seal the entrance with a rucksack.

Building low walls sounds easy but it requires some skill and practice (see p. 21). Every stone laid should sit on at least two other stones to 'tie' them together. The stones should be shuffled about so that they sit firmly on the other stones and do not wobble. Smaller flat or wedge-shaped stones can be used as 'chocks' to prevent wobble. It is often a good idea to stuff dead grass or bracken into any large holes as the wall is being built.

Camping and bivouacking in summer, especially near trees and water, is often marred by midges and other biting or stinging insects.

19

Wall shelters with plastic roof

a A low wall shelter with plastic roof, using a pack frame as a central support to let water run off (could be a stick, ice-axe or anything similar available). Remember to make the entrance on the sheltered or down-wind side. Another pack frame can be used to seal off the entrance

wind direction

c Low-profile shelter for windy conditions

b Another type of wall shelter, with the roof stretched between two walls

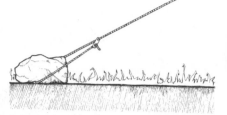

d Large heavy stone holds the string

f Chockstone anchor in rock cleft. A large knot at the end of the cord can also be used

How to secure your poly sheet

a Push a small stone, pebble, ball of grass or similar into the plastic and twist it round to make a 'neck'. Tie string or cord tightly round the neck

b One way of keeping the polythene in place in a simple summer-time shelter between trees

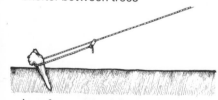

c In soft ground, sticks and twigs can be used instead of tent pegs

e In very soft ground such as sand, snow or peat, make a 'dead-man' anchor by burying the guy-line. Dig out a trench for the stick (could be driftwood or a bundle of reeds – tent pegs are usually too small). Make a slit out of one side to accommodate the guy-rope. Carefully fill in the trench and slit, and tamp down firmly with hand or foot

through-stone

g Dry-stone walling. Lay biggest stones at bottom, and a 'through-stone' here and there to help 'tie' the wall together. Every stone should 'lock-in' at least two others. If possible use a substantial top stone to round off the wall. At the corners use bigger stones facing alternate ways to key the two walls together

Winter bivouac in a snowdrift (this snow was unsuitable for making blocks)

Living under the sky in summer time without a shelter. An Eskimo pile fabric sleeping bag is being used

These are usually most troublesome at dawn and dusk. For protection against midge bites use midge-repellent creams or spray-on anti-midge solutions. Most of these are fairly effective. Follow carefully the instructions on the product. Cover up as much skin area as you can. Inside the tent or 'bivvy' you can burn a proprietary anti-insect coil. These coils smoulder away slowly, giving off a fragrant smell which seems to discourage most midges and other troublesome flies. They are inexpensive and useful.

A sophisticated and original mountain bivouac – note the location and distribution of anchor points; no pegs were used

3 Progress in easy stages

When you have mastered some of the rudiments of walking, cooking and sleeping out in the open with relatively simple and cheap equipment you can progress gradually on to more demanding and ambitious projects.

First, try to improve your level of fitness and stamina. Do longer one-day hikes. The Three Peaks of Yorkshire walk – 23 miles (37km) and 4,500ft (1,384m) of ascent – is a classic for people living in the North of England. Many similar walks exist up and down the country and you can get further information from organisations such as the Ramblers Association and the Long Distance Walkers Association (see p. 115 for addresses). The 'Ramblers' have local and regional groups. Further information can be gleaned by watching the local press, visiting your local library or studying the Club Notes sections of the outdoor magazines (see p. 119).

Build up your mileage gradually. This will avoid sore feet and stiff limbs. You will soon be amazed at how far you can walk in one day if you build up to it sensibly. Your map reading and navigation skills will also improve with practice. Of course at first you must attempt these long walks only in the summer time when the daylight hours are long. Later with more experience and fitness you can try harder walks in winter. Remember, however, that the weather can be quite severe in the winter months. Proper clothing and route planning (see later chapters) must be observed if you are to keep out of trouble. A moderately long summer walk can easily become an epic if attempted in the winter time. You should be off the hills and safely in the valleys by nightfall.

Night walks

However, having given the standard piece of advice it is a good idea to attempt some night-hikes. Darkness brings a completely new dimension to a familiar walk in open country. Nothing looks the same.

B

Night navigation

There are no colours. Obvious paths in the daytime sometimes become almost invisible at night even with a torch. This applies especially to green paths which seem so well-defined in daylight. They are easily seen because of their different shade of green. In the darkness, colour differences disappear.

To begin with, attempt such walks with your friends and follow familiar routes. Keep away from farms and habitation. You should not disturb people's sleep with your interesting activities. Farm dogs will detect your presence in agricultural areas, barking a warning to their owners in good time. Do not antagonise country folk in this way. Woods, downs, moorlands, beaches and a host of other places offer plenty of scope for night navigation practice without disturbing anyone.

Midnight hikes have a great fascination for young people – and for some old people I know who have been doing them for a lifetime (midnight ramblers). They are exciting, adventurous (usually quite innocuous) and sometimes a little 'scary'. The moon, or lack of it, makes a great contribution. For many urbanites their first real look at the stars is on a midnight walk miles away from the glare of town and city street lights. The 'acid test' of navigation is to be on a moor at the dead of night in a thick fog. Make sure you choose an area free of hazards such as cliffs and disused mine shafts. Remember to take or wear the following:

- ☐ Good torch, plus spare bulb and batteries (three high-powered U2 batteries will only give four hours of continuous light)
- ☐ Map and compass (keep the torch away from the compass as it will deflect the needle)
- ☐ Food and Thermos or stove for making hot food and drink
- ☐ Whistle
- ☐ Warm clothing (include woolly hat and gloves)
- ☐ Waterproof clothing (jacket and trousers)
- ☐ 'Bivvy' bag or sheet (you may have to wait until dawn if you get lost)
- ☐ First aid equipment

Finding your way across rough country in the dark can be a great challenge. It can give a great sense of achievement if accomplished successfully. Further, it engenders confidence in one's ability as well as highlighting the need to be off serious ground (mountains and complex or dangerous areas) before nightfall. The art of night navigation in hilly country is a great asset and improves one's safety margin tremendously. *A word of warning.* Plan the route carefully. At first only travel over *known* ground. Go with reliable companions – no passengers. Every person should have at least one good torch. It is very unsatisfactory to have to share a light especially over rough ground. If anything, extra lights should be carried as well as spare batteries and bulbs. Take the equipment as listed. Finally make sure that a reliable person or parent knows *exactly* what your plans are, where you are going and your estimated time of return. Stick to your plan. Your arrangements should include emergency plans, escape routes (in case of bad weather), check or message points (to be collected later) and the telephone number of your friend or parent. Carry some coins with you or reverse the charges by arrangement. You have a duty to keep people informed of your progress where this is possible, to inform them of a change of plan for whatever reason and ideally to let them know the walk is completed and that you have reached a safe place (bus stop, train, car etc.). There is no excuse for causing needless worry and alarm through mere thoughtlessness. Also remember that no-one, absolutely no-one, is going to thank you if you make a mess of it. 'Minimum impact' in this context means that you only contact the police and rescue teams as a last resort. Begin in a modest way, build up experience gradually and progressively and all should be well. Realise there is no such thing as an 'instant' hill-walker, backpacker or mountaineer. Only time and experience can create such people.

Solo expeditions ('the inward journey')

At the risk of criticism from some quarters one should consider solo trips. Amongst the *good* advice normally handed out to everyone, especially young people, is that which says *Never Go Alone*. Well, that is too dogmatic. Anyone who frequents the British hills will tell you that the solitary walker is a feature of the scenery. To condemn the solitary walker, mountaineer or backpacker is really an expression of ignorance of what solitude, freedom and spiritual contact with nature is all about. It does not appeal to everyone, but for many of us there are times when we like to share the hills with our friends and there are times when we like to be alone with the wind, rain and wide open spaces. It can be very therapeutic. Obviously the risks are bigger and the stakes higher but the rewards are greater. One gets to know oneself the better in such circumstances.

Solo walks should be planned with infinite care. It is even more important that you inform someone of your route, leave intermediate messages (giving time, condition and any variation of plan) at previously arranged points and at the end of the day telephone someone stating your whereabouts if you are not returning home that evening. The last point is particularly important if you are doing a solo walk of, say, the Pennine Way. If you were incapacitated in the first day or two no-one would know anything was wrong until you failed to turn up at home two weeks later! The solitary walker is occasionally found dead on the hills (often through natural causes) but is rarely the subject of a rescue. Most rescues are for groups of people. The solo walker takes more care, is more cautious and takes less risks because he knows the likely consequences of a mistake. You must carry all the essential items to ensure your survival as far as is possible, in wilderness areas. With the right equipment (see below) you could probably survive an accident or injury, even sickness, long enough to be missed and therefore discovered and rescued. The one big fear is that you may slip and be knocked unconscious, in which case any amount of survival gear in your rucksack will be of no help to you unless you come round sufficiently to be able to use it.

Solo walker's survival equipment in use

In winter and remote areas carry a two-man size polythene bag (8 x 4ft – 2.44 x 1.22m), coloured orange if possible (or wear bright clothing). (N.B. Use *thick* polythene; very thin polythene clings and could suffocate you.) If you need to make an emergency bivouac, position yourself where you can easily be seen by people on the expected line of approach, but in a sheltered place. Face away from the wind, with all clothing on under duvet or sleeping bag, feet in rucksack and insulating mat beneath. Whistle, flask, torch, food should all be within easy reach.

In a polythene bag this size it is easy to sit up at one end and normally there is enough ventilation due to the bellows effect of the wind blowing the polythene about. It is simple to get dressed in the bag.

The best heat-conserving shape is sitting curled up like a ball – the foetal position. Wear *all* clothing underneath waterproofs to create as many layers of air as possible, plus woollen Balaclava and mittens. Tuck feet into rucksack and ensure that all vital items of equipment – food, flask, whistle, torch – are near to hand. Sit on insulating mat and pull polythene bag round head, leaving small opening for face.

If in trouble, blow whistle frequently. Use the Alpine Distress Signal – six long blasts. Or flash your torch – six flashes, pause, six flashes, pause etc.

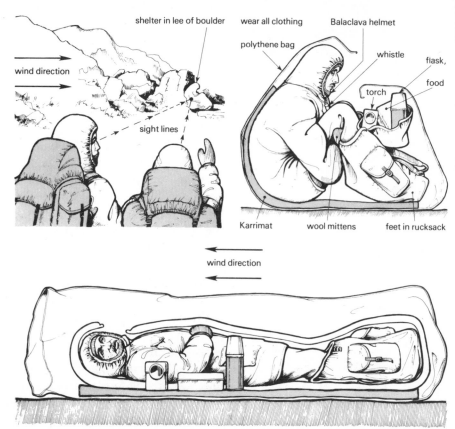

shelter in lee of boulder

wind direction

sight lines

wear all clothing

Balaclava helmet

polythene bag

whistle

flask, food

torch

Karrimat

wool mittens

feet in rucksack

wind direction

An emergency bivouac

Sooner or later everyone should try a solo journey, sleeping out in a quiet place overnight a long way from people, using either a bivouac or a tent. It is often a salutary experience – certainly an educative one. However, it cannot be too strongly emphasised that you should acquire this kind of experience gradually over a long period of time. At first, attempt easy things in the summer on easy ground, then on more difficult terrain, then maybe a night walk on easy ground in summer. Slowly graduate to doing similar things in the winter on known ground. If you go solo night walking in winter and bad weather, you could be pushing your luck, depending on the type of area you are in. From here it's only a short step to mad foolhardiness which cannot be justified.

Multiple-night bivouacking in summer

Almost anyone can enjoy, put up with or suffer one night in a temporary shelter. The real test of competence is to do a journey on foot, spending several nights in succession bivouacking. This is not too difficult if the weather is fine. Some people do long-distance footpaths in this fashion. But only those who have mastered the basic skills of bivouacking can cope with several days and nights of wet weather.

As with multiple-night camping the most important thing is to keep your sleeping bag dry, especially if it's a down-filled one. Some sleeping bags perform quite well when wet (see p. 53), though better when dry. As a general principle the sleeping bag must be kept dry. Also aim to keep one set of clothes dry to sleep in. If you eat well and have a dry bed then you are unlikely to take much harm. Masochistic as it may seem it is better to put one's wet clothes on again in the morning rather than risk wetting the remaining dry set. You will need the dry clothes at the end of the day to wear inside your tent or bivouac and to sleep in. It is foolish and short-sighted to get *all* your clothes wet. They are much heavier to carry, too. During spells of fine weather hang wet clothing on the outside of your rucksack to dry whilst you are walking.

Most sleeping bags are sold together with a 'stuff-sack'. Many of these are made of proofed materials but cannot be relied upon to keep your sleeping bag dry in very wet weather. You must also pack it in a medium-gauge polythene bag of adequate dimensions so that you can twist or fold the neck to keep out rain and moisture. Remember there is no such thing as a completely waterproof rucksack: wind-driven rain and Scotch mist percolate their way into the best of rucksacks. (You have been warned.) Adopt a 'belt-and-braces' attitude to keeping your clothes and sleeping bag dry.

On arrival at your overnight site, first make a 'brew' and construct your bivouac depending on circumstance. By now you should have had adequate practice at this. Do not unpack your sleeping bag until you need to get into it, otherwise it will pick up moisture and wetness and lose some, if not all, of its efficiency. In the morning if it is still raining, then pack your sleeping bag away in its waterproof wrappers as soon as you get out of it. Try to keep it dry at all costs. If the weather is fine and conditions permit try to air your sleeping bag before packing it away. This can be done by draping it over your 'bivvy' or over a fence, wall, branch of tree or something similar. Have a very good nourishing breakfast and plenty to drink. Strike camp (i.e., take down the 'bivvy'), pack your rucksack and check the area. Leave no traces of your stay and start out on the next leg of your journey. Remember the worse the weather the better your breakfast should be. Have plenty of hot drinks.

Winter walking
First a word about walking in the cold winter time. Do not be too ambitious. Wet soggy ground, mud and snow make the going strenuous and at times exhausting. Generally, you will be carrying more weight (extra clothes, food and equipment) which puts further demands on your energy. The weather may be against you: strong winds, low temperatures and poor visibility (mist, rain, snow or early nightfall).

In certain winter conditions speeds of one mile per hour are not uncommon.

Winter bivouacking
This should be done with caution and only after you have had plenty of experience of bivouacking. If you can cope with multiple-night bivouacking in poor summer weather then you should be ready to meet the challenges of winter bivouacking. As usual you must try this out in a relatively safe place, not too far from habitation. Later you may feel competent to go into more remote areas. It is best to go with

Emergency bivouac in wintry conditions

Winter backpacking in snow is a serious business

a friend or friends as the winter nights are very long and the daylight hours short, leaving little time for shelter construction.

Superior clothing, sleeping bags and sleeping mats are imperative. Thick woollen mitts are a must as the raw building materials will be very cold to handle and use. A good reliable stove and plenty of food are equally important. You should be quite expert by now if you have gone through the progressions recommended in this book. The main hazards of winter bivouacking are obvious – low temperatures, strong winds, possibilty of snow and long hours of darkness. Holes should be plugged to keep out cold draughts and powdered snow. Go to a lot of trouble to ensure the wind does not rip your roof off in the middle of the night.

A section on winter bivouacking would not be complete without some reference to the use of snow as a building material. This is often referred to as 'snow-holing' or the building of snow shelters (igloos). It can be tremendous fun, a life-saving technique, strenuous, technically very interesting as snow is an infinitely variable material, and it can be fatally simple or simply fatal to the ill-informed.

The main hazards are foul air, collapse of shelter due to melting and getting clothes and bedding wet. Adequate ventilation must be ensured at all times – normally one opening left at the doorway coupled with a ventilation hole in the roof. Great care must be taken to prevent the build up of carbon monoxide (CO) and carbon dioxide (CO_2). These are usually the by-products of combustion. The cooking stove and candle are the obvious sources in this case. The stove and candle also burn up valuable oxygen as do we ourselves (we also breathe out CO_2). Obviously good ventilation is imperative not only to get rid of harmful gases but to ensure an adequate supply of life-supporting oxygen. This cannot be stressed too much. There have been a number of fatalities in snow holes due to the lack of proper ventilation, as indeed there have been in other improvised shelters such as vans, caravans, boats and tents buried in snow. Normally it happens in cold weather when people seal up all the holes and have a stove burning inside for warmth and cooking. Unfortunately it is not easy to detect for oneself oxygen lack or excess carbon monoxide; both have a soporific effect. Drowsiness may be due to the effects of a good meal after a strenuous day and not due to bad air, but be on your guard. Watch the ventilation aspects of your shelter. Too much carbon dioxide usually shows itself by an increase in the rate of breathing. If you start panting for no obvious reason then there is almost certainly too much CO_2 in the atmosphere. I know of two people who once sat in a snow hole watching their candle flame getting smaller and smaller and couldn't work out why. Happily they realised before it was too late that their ventilation holes had become blocked by a heavy fall of snow.

Instead of using a candle for illumination consider using a chemical light. They are excellent in a snow hole as you can stick them into the walls or roof anywhere. They give off a green fluorescent-type light and remain completely cold: one of the original proprietary names was Coolite. Basically its two chemicals, when mixed together, react to give off light. One chemical is inside a rigid glass tube or phial which is then placed inside a flexible plastic tube containing the other chemical. The once-and-for-all switch-on is made by breaking the glass tube inside by bending the outer plastic sleeve, thus bringing the two chemicals into contact. Unfortunately these lights are fairly expensive and occasionally do not work. However, when functioning properly they give off light for anything up to 24 hours. They are completely safe to use in confined spaces and cannot be extinguished.

Getting wet is a major problem when using snow as a building material. It can be fairly heavy stuff and handling large quantities of it is very strenuous. Guard against over-heating (sweating) when digging snow holes or cutting and carrying snow blocks. Also snow particles on and in the clothing will subsequently melt with body heat. Either way your insulating layers of clothing are going to get wet. Later on this clothing is going to feel cold and clammy and might even freeze (see pp. 67-74 on clothing). In most circumstances, it is best to remove as much warm clothing as possible and store it in your rucksack, thus keeping it dry whilst you do the strenuous work. When the activity stops replace the sweaters and shirts to keep warm.

The best way to learn is to make a practice snow hole or shelter as an activity on one of your day walks in the winter. Make lunch in it; you will learn a lot. Really you should do this two or three times before seriously considering spending a night in such a shelter. There is hardly any friction between snow and polythene; if there is snow on the ground, exercise extreme caution or you will slide down the hill in your polythene bag!

Practise making shelters whenever you can (there is a lot to learn)

31

A snow hole inside (note equipment) ...

... and outside

Once inside your ice-palace, move about cautiously. Try not to touch the walls and roof to avoid dislodging snow and ice particles on to your clothing, which will subsequently become wet. Smooth off the inside of the shelter to avoid drips. As far as possible keep the temperature in your snow house below freezing, otherwise you may be troubled with drips of water or, more importantly, it may melt and collapse on you. In changeable weather conditions when a sudden thaw is likely, have alternative bivouacking materials to hand.

Another interesting problem is preventing your cooking stove and its contents from falling over. The heat of the stove acts as a thermal lance, slowly melting a hole underneath itself. Often, suddenly and without warning, a stove and pan of hot soup topple sideways into the snow – disappointing and could be dangerous, producing nasty scalds. One way to avoid this is to put your wet mittens or socks under the stove. This stops the snow from melting and helps to dry them out a little.

Snow saws and portable collapsible shovels are the main tools used in making snow houses. Ice axes, hands, feet, cooking pots and sundry other items are sometimes called into use as well. The main thing is to practise various constructions. All you need is some common sense, imagination and energy.

Snow bivouacs: a one-man shelter cut out of a snow bank
a Sitting up in a sleeping bag and cooking
b Sleeping, all gear inside, torch and digging equipment close by

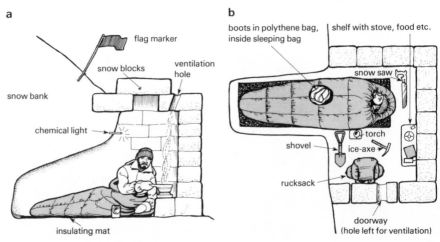

a

flag marker

snow blocks

ventilation hole

snow bank

chemical light

insulating mat

b

boots in polythene bag, inside sleeping bag | shelf with stove, food etc.

snow saw

torch

shovel

ice-axe

rucksack

doorway
(hole left for ventilation)

ground level

a

Two- and three-man shelters

a Igloo. Build with snow blocks in a spiral, base 8ft (2.44m) in diameter inside (1). The builder trims and makes blocks a good fit by passing saw backwards and forwards between them and pushing from the side. Fill and pack any holes with snow on the outside. Lower the top block into place (2). **One man** should be outside **the shelter – he can** then cut a doorway and make an entrance (3). Scrape the inside with a shovel to smooth off any projections which may drip water on to you, due to heat from stove and people. A trench at the tunnel entrance makes access easier (4). Remember to make a ventilation hole. The completed igloo (5)

b Cut trench into snow bank, pulling out spoil on polythene sheet and throwing it away downhill (1). Cut out sleeping shelves about 3ft (90cm) wide at sides (2). Close entrance with snow block wall (3). Cut a low entrance hole in the wall and a ventilation hole in the top. Set a coloured flag stick over the shelter (4). If more than one snow hole, link them together with a rope, otherwise you may not find your friends after a fall of snow

b

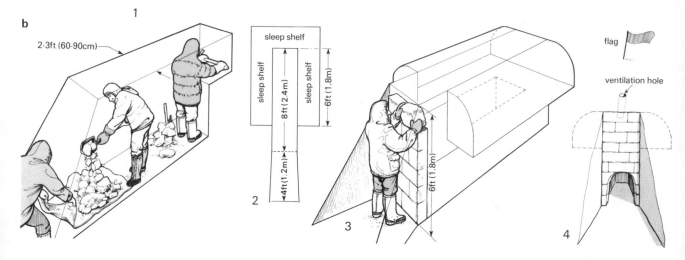

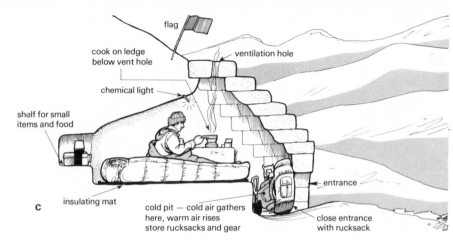

c

flag

cook on ledge
below vent hole

ventilation hole

chemical light

shelf for small
items and food

entrance

insulating mat

cold pit — cold air gathers
here, warm air rises
store rucksacks and gear

close entrance
with rucksack

c Combined snow cave and igloo. Dig
a cave in a snow bank and wall up
entrance. In a confined space it is
better if one cooks and the others lie
still, taking turns with meals

d Snowballs. Roll large snowballs
down slope to level ground and
assemble to make shelters or cut
into blocks. For shelters, pack snow
between the snowballs and hollow
out

d

Always take the obvious precautions:
- ☐ Mark your site, if not obvious, with a stick (flag) to
  prevent others falling through it
- ☐ Choose stable, consolidated snow slopes
- ☐ Take everything inside with you, especially digging tools. You
  may have to dig your way out
- ☐ If you leave your shelter after dark, even for a short distance,
  leave a light at the entrance, otherwise you may not find it again
- ☐ Ensure that *adequate ventilation* is maintained all the time
- ☐ Put your boots in a polythene bag and keep them in bed with
  you to prevent freezing

34

Warning If you venture far out of the valleys in winter time, remember that winter conditions on hills require specialised knowledge and equipment, e.g. crampons and an ice-axe. The use of such equipment is outside the scope of this book. Study books on winter mountaineering and seek specialist training if you want to visit the mountains in winter.

Remember – *there is no substitute for knowledge and experience.*

a

b

c

d

a Choose a safe slope – not too steep and away from avalanche risk
b Strenuous work
c Working from the inside. Note a snow block quarry in foreground
d The finished snow house

35

Travelling through the Teton range of
the Rocky Mountains

4 Techniques

Navigation with map and compass

Learn to understand and use a map as soon as possible. Most people have a fair understanding of maps already. The 'key' on the map gives the scale, for instance 1 inch = 1 mile : 2cm = 1km (1:50,000), and tells you what the symbols mean. All Ordnance Survey maps have a grid system of squares superimposed over them. Each square represents one kilometre no matter what scale the map is made to. This is a great help in judging distances without actually measuring them. The grid is a system whereby any point in Britain can be identified to the nearest hundred metres, by a number. This number is called a grid reference. For most practical purposes it is a six figure number. The grid reference is a very useful and unambiguous method of identifying places you intend to visit and for conveying beyond doubt to other people points on a map or indeed places on the ground. Make sure you get the numbers in the correct order. First read the numbers along the bottom of the map, then up the side. An easy way to remember this is: 'Along the passage, up the stairs'.

The map, a flat two-dimensional piece of paper, tries to show a solid three-dimensional area of land. (Some complex mountainous areas, such as the Cuillin Ridge in Skye, are almost impossible for even the cartographer's skill to represent on a flat sheet of paper.) The recognised technique for showing the vertical element of the land-scape is by the use of contour lines. Contour lines are lines on a map connecting together a series of points which are exactly the same height above sea level. If this is repeated at different heights above sea level we get a series of lines depicting the shape of the ground (see diagram). The vertical distance between the lines varies according to the scale and quality of the map. The map key indicates what the vertical interval is on that particular map. It takes quite a lot of practice to be able to visualise the bumps and hollows (hills and valleys) by simply looking at the map. Being able to recognise land

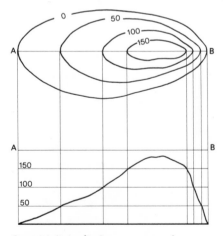

Contour lines (in feet or metres) indicate height above sea level and long or steep slopes

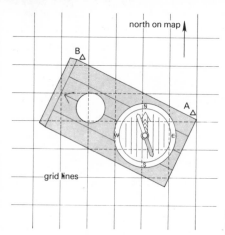

north on map

B

A

grid lines

How to work out a bearing from A to B. Line up the edge of the compass between the two points (note direction of travel). Turn bezel so that arrow in base is in line with grid lines, pointing north on map. Add on 'x' degrees (values are given on the map) for the difference between magnetic and grid north

Walk a triangle for compass practice

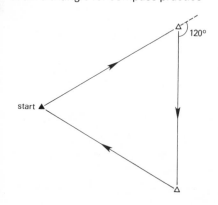

120°

start

forms (spurs, corries, concave and convex slopes) from a flat map is the hallmark of a good map-reader.

In order to be able to 'navigate', which is what sailors do on the featureless sea (not unlike being on land in a thick mist or darkness), a compass is required. As suggested earlier, it is wise to buy a Silva-type liquid-filled compass, with a rectangular perspex base. The liquid prevents the magnetic needle from oscillating wildly. Other kinds are useless for accurate work. The base, together with the graduated revolving bezel, forms a protractor for working out bearings (see diagram). The compass can also be used to set or orientate the map so that it relates to the ground.

Having worked out on the map a bearing you wish to follow, the next thing is to put it into practice on the ground. Hold the baseplate of the compass in one hand and turn round until the magnetic needle is in line with the arrow on the bottom of the needle housing. Make sure you have the *north end* of the needle (usually red in colour) in the arrowhead – otherwise you will start travelling in the opposite direction from the one you wish to go. Once everything is lined up correctly you are ready to travel. Walking and looking at the compass simultaneously is not very accurate and you may walk over a cliff or into a bog while you are doing it. The best way is to look along the compass in the line of travel, identify some recognisable object not too far away, such as a tree, shrub or rock, and then walk to it by the easiest route. Once there repeat the manoeuvre until you have covered the necessary distance to reach your objective.

'Compass marching' needs lots of practice and learning can be good fun. For example, choose some safe but rough ground (moorland, heath, woods) and test out your ability to travel (navigate) accurately using only a compass. Put a small object down on the ground, say a 50p piece. Choose any bearing at random and using your compass travel about 100 yards (90m). Stop, add 120°, walk the same distance again, do the same yet again and you should arrive back at your 50p piece having walked an equilateral triangle (see diagram). Try other shapes – a square or a rectangle. Increase the distances as you improve. Another way is to find a moorland road or track. Leave a small marker at the roadside and set off on a bearing across country for a given distance. Stop, turn round and by using your compass with the needle reversed in its alignment (this gives a reciprocal bearing) walk back again. You can test the accuracy of your navigation by seeing how far you are away from your marker on reaching the road again. If you are within ten yards (9m) then you are quite good.

Practice navigating with a friend in poor visibility or darkness. Choose a safe featureless place. One person sets off on the bearing for a short distance, the other looking along his compass shouts corrective instructions: 'right-a-bit', 'left-a-bit'. The first person stops before he goes out of view to be then joined by his friend. Keep on repeating the procedure until the required distance has been covered. If time is important then the same principle can be applied on the move. Both people walk a safe distance apart using their compasses on the same bearing. The person at the back calls out corrective instructions as necessary.

Travelling in a straight line without compasses, using the 'chain-marching' technique

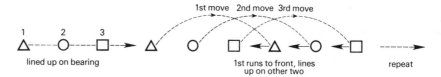

If there are three people or more then it is possible to travel in a straight line without using compasses by a leap-frogging routine (see diagram above). First three people line up on the bearing, say 20 yards (18m) apart, to make a straight line. Only one person at a time must move otherwise the system breaks down. It is a very accurate method, sometimes called 'chain-marching' and need not be too slow if the back person always runs to the front.

Good navigation relies on travelling accurately on a bearing for the correct distance. Estimating and measuring distance can be difficult. For distances up to 400 or 500 yards or metres counting paces is accurate. You need to check how many of your normal paces make up a set distance. Distances greater than this are best dealt with on a time and motion basis. With practice you know what walking at 3 miles or 5km an hour feels like. This means a mile in twenty minutes, half a mile in ten minutes, and a quarter of a mile in five minutes. Of course you need a watch to achieve any sort of accuracy, and plenty of practice.

You can improve your navigation and compass work tremendously by doing some orienteering. In some places permanent courses are

Beginners marking down the route on a simple orienteering course

laid out so that you do them anytime for fun and practice. Most areas have orienteering events to suit everybody, novices, experts, young, old and family groups. They naturally vary in length and difficulty. Information can be obtained from the British Orienteering Federation (address on p. 115).

Route planning

It was recommended in the introductory chapters on bivouacking that you progress steadily in easy stages. However, routes should be planned which are realistic. A rather effective if somewhat crude formula (Naismith's Rule) is to measure the horizontal distance and assume a speed of 3 miles per hour, work out the height gain and add half an hour for every 1,000ft. The result is the likely time it will take you. It is important that, in the beginning at least, you do this throughly for every section of the journey. Of course Naismith's Rule does not allow for stops to admire the view, consult a map or a break for refreshments. You must include some time for this yourself.

When backpacking with a heavy load the formula changes to $2\frac{1}{2}$ miles an hour for distance and three-quarters of an hour for every 1,000ft of ascent. The metric equivalent for Naismith's Rule is: without heavy load – 4km per hour for horizontal distance, half an hour for 300m of ascent; with a heavy load – 3km per hour for horizontal distance, three-quarters of an hour for 300m of ascent.

Obviously Naismith's Rule is a rough guide and much depends on your own physical fitness, the terrain, the weather (strong winds, mist) and your companions. In bad conditions speed can be reduced to 1 mile per hour.

When route planning study the map carefully; it tells you a lot but not everything. Seek local knowledge and advice if you do not know the area. In hilly country try to choose the easiest gradients, keep away from danger spots (crags), take the least line of resistance, especially if carrying a load. Work out likely stopping places for lunch or breaks, near a spring or stream, or a place with a good view. Also work out 'escape routes' when visiting the hills. This means places where you can easily get down to safety if the weather gets too bad, or you become too tired or maybe darkness approaches. If there is any kind of emergency it is good to know beforehand where the easy descents are.

Have a checklist (see end of Chapter 5) made out the day before to make sure that you will not leave some vital item behind (woolly hat, food, whistle etc.). Write down your route and make sure that some responsible person knows what your plans are and what time you expect to be back. Make every effort to honour your final deadline – otherwise police and rescue teams are put to considerable inconvenience.

Finally, before you go listen to the weather forecast and modify your route if necessary. Many people plan two routes, fine and bad weather ones. Let your 'contact' know which route you are taking.

Hill-walking skills
Any kind of sustained walking demands a steady pace and rhythm. This is especially true of hill-walking when carrying a loaded rucksack. Start out at a speed you know you can keep up for a few hours at least, if not all day. If you cannot walk and talk then you are probably travelling too fast. Solo backpackers should be able to whistle and walk (talking to oneself out loud could be misinterpreted). Newcomers to hill climbing need to be reminded that hills are climbed by putting one foot in front of the other. No matter how small the step, it is a step nearer the summit. Stopping for whatever

41

reason gets you nowhere. Too many stops interfere with the rhythm; the steady slow mechanical plod is amazingly efficient and effective. It is surprising how quickly height is gained and the summit reached.

The steady plod also prevents overheating, and sweating, which wets the clothing and contributes to dehydration as well as chilling when finally you reach the summit. Stop-go-stop walkers soon tire and usually fatigue badly later in the day. Wise hillmen conserve their energy and stay in good condition, not tiring themselves and not getting too hot or too cold. Constant adjustment of speed and clothing bring this about, plus the elimination of unnecessary stops.

Ascending a hill

If your calf muscles ache a lot going up hills then you are probably not placing your feet very well on the hillside. The chances are that you are pointing your feet directly up the slope putting tremendous strain on your calf muscles and Achilles tendon. Try walking up the hill in a series of zig-zags. This enables the foot to be placed across the slope, taking a lot of strain off the lower leg. It also enables the boot to have more contact with the ground, reducing the likelihood of a slip. 'Tacking' up the hillside effectively reduces the gradient by taking longer to gain the same amount of height as a direct ascent and is therefore less tiring. Always try to keep your feet as horizontal as possible by carefully placing them on indentations or bits of rock. Whenever possible take two steps instead of one to avoid straining joints and ligaments. It also uses less energy.

Foot placement on hill

a Incorrect walking straight up a hill with large steps and feet badly positioned (boot not making much contact with ground, and thrusting down at an angle) puts tremendous strain on the legs, throws the body out of balance, and uses up a lot of energy. There is danger of slipping as well

b The correct way is to walk with small steps and feet across the slope (boot in good contact with ground, and thrusting straight down) to conserve energy and reduce strain

Descending a slope Running down hills can be good fun, though it can also be dangerous and tiring. On the other hand some people are too timid descending a steep slope. Care should be taken not to slip. Carrying a heavy pack downhill requires a bit of technique. It is difficult to generalise. What is steep to one person is an easy slope to another. It all depends what you are used to.

As a general principle it is better to adopt a dynamic posture and a positive attitude to steep descents no matter what your standards are. The main thing is to bend both your knees and lean well forward. The bent legs act as springs or shock absorbers to reduce the shaking-up of the body which many people experience going down hill. Leaning forward ensures that if a foot does slip you do not fall backwards. The backside was never designed as a mode of travel and sliding down the hillside on it can be very dangerous. If a diagonal or sideways descent is made in this gorilla-like posture then the uphill hand must be very close to the ground to assist stability. When carrying a heavy load keep off scree slopes – most in Britain are worn out anyway. If a steep slope frightens you too much find an easier way down.

Dynamic posture, weight slightly in front of feet . . .
. . . prevents you from slipping and falling backwards

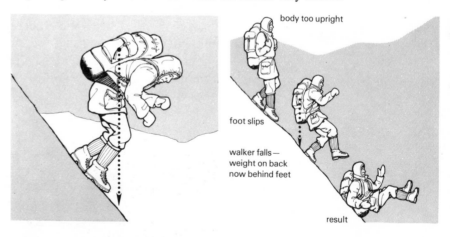

body too upright

foot slips

walker falls—
weight on back
now behind feet

result

Crossing rivers and mountain streams The best advice is, never cross a river or mountain stream in flood. Moving water is very powerful and inexperienced people nearly always under-estimate its force.

However, it is often reasonable and safe to cross streams and small rivers. In winter the main thing is to avoid an immersion even in one foot of water which may have come from melting snows higher up

Crossing a river by the 'third-leg' method

and will therefore be very cold. Getting soaked by falling into relatively shallow water in cold winter weather could prove disastrous (see pp. 97-98 on temperature regulation and hypothermia), apart from being very uncomfortable.

The main thing is to create a stable base for yourself whilst you cross the rounded slippery stones below the water. You can do this by creating a 'third leg' with a stout stick or pole, though they are never easy to come by when you want one. Face upstream so that any water pressure will not buckle your knees. Lean on the stick to make a tripod. Move the stick and each leg one at a time to cross the water (see left).

If there are two people, face each other legs wide apart and with arms outstretched, lean on each other a little. Enter the water with one hip facing upstream to reduce drag and shuffle across taking short steps.

Three people is the best arrangement. Make a tripod, legs wide apart to create a broad base, lean towards each other at the top to form a sort of rugby scrum (see photograph below). Enter the water so that one person is facing upstream, so that the water presses on the front of their legs with the others presenting one side to the current.

In all cases of crossing water undo waist belts and carry heavy packs on one shoulder so that they can be jettisoned in an emergency. (A living person without a pack is better than a drowned person with one.)

River crossing in winter by tripod technique

5 Equipment

Tents

Up to now we have concentrated on living in bivouacs or improvised shelters partly as a means of saving money though more importantly as training in a basic survival technique, encouraging self-reliance, initiative and enterprise. Hopefully it has been good fun and at times adventurous. However, you will also have realised that bivouacking has a number of drawbacks. It is very time-consuming, often strenuous, and in many ways unpredictable. Obviously if you want to spend more time walking and seeing things, or if you want a more predictable and less draughty shelter, then some form of tent is the answer. It will cost you money and you will have to carry it all day but you can erect it in a few minutes.

The dividing line between a bivouac and a tent is very blurred indeed. When does a polythene bag become a primitive tent or a simple tent a glorified bag? It is possible to buy a 'bivouac tent'; these are usually very light one-man tents made of impervious material and extremely small – really a portable bivouac. For practical purposes there is not much difference between these and a large polythene bag. One definition of a tent is 'A portable shelter made of fabric which is supported by means of a pole or poles and usually extended and secured by cords fastened to pegs which are driven into the ground'. There are of course variations to this definition.

At a recent exhibition I counted over ninety lightweight tents which were suitable for some form of backpacking. Tents are made in an amazing range of shapes, sizes and materials. There is intense competition between the manufacturers to produce the 'ideal' tent for backpackers at a reasonable price. This is good for us – the consumers. However, you will be faced with a bewildering choice when you decide to buy. No-one can tell you which is the best tent for you. It has to be a personal choice. What you finally choose to purchase in the way of backpacking equipment is the result of a complicated

45

equation which relates weight to comfort to cost to the kind of activity you envisage. Weight and comfort are inextricably related. The more gear you carry the higher the degree of comfort in camp but the greater the discomfort en route. Only you can decide. Financial consideration will affect the kind of equipment you can afford to buy. Winter backpacking in the hills demands better, more expensive equipment than summer backpacking in the valleys. Your equipment may be the limiting factor on what it is safe to do. You can pay anything between £20 and £120 plus for a tent.

Some designers and manufacturers make extravagant claims for their tents. Rely on your own judgement. You should have learned a lot about shelter design if you have been bivouacking. Mostly you get what you pay for but it does not follow that an expensive tent is necessarily a good one. Have a good look around to see what there is. Talk to people in camp sites about the pros and cons of their tents. Pick other people's brains about equipment. Go to a reputable outdoor shop if you can but don't take their word as gospel.

Tents (portable homes) are made of relatively weak materials (fabrics) compared to permanent homes which are made of strong rigid materials (bricks, concrete and wood). It follows therefore that they are bound to have some limitations. No structural engineer would choose a thin fabric as an appropriate building material for a storm shelter. The tent designers and manufacturers do a very good job and many claim that their specially designed mountain tents will stand up in gale force winds and bad weather. Some do and some don't.

Never under-estimate the power of the wind or over-estimate the strength of your tent. Whenever possible, study the lie of the land for a good site, well drained, reasonably level and sheltered from the wind. If in windy locations, hills, mountains or at the coast, then assume that a gale is going to blow in the night. Pitch your tent carefully and reinforce the pegs and guy lines with natural materials. Also make some kind of wind-break (see photograph on p. 47). The cheaper and less sophisticated your tent the more important it is that you help it to survive strong winds. Better to carry out this work in daylight or before you turn in, rather than to have to get out in the middle of the night in driving rain to fix your tent by torchlight. Alternatively your tent may just collapse on you without warning.

If possible, find a sheltered site for your tent

Build a low wall to protect your tent in case a gale blows in the night

The experience will make you a wiser person. Camping is a very practical thing and cannot easily be learnt from a book.

Fundamentally a tent protects you from the climate, against the wind, rain, snow, sun, insects and prying eyes. These attributes vary in importance depending on the time of year and place in which you travel. There are dozens of different designs of tent but most fall into one of five basic shapes: ridge, pyramid, cone, tunnel and wedge. Some different types are shown below. Naturally there are many variations and combinations both in plan and elevation.

Tent designs are determined by three main factors: enclosed

Tent types

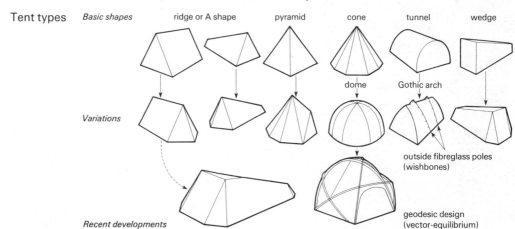

Basic shapes — ridge or A shape — pyramid — cone — tunnel — wedge

dome — Gothic arch

Variations

outside fibreglass poles (wishbones)

Recent developments

geodesic design (vector-equilibrium)

c

47

usable space, weight and cost. Weight and cost are closely related to usable volume. Normally the smaller the tent the less it weighs and the less it costs. Uncomplicated designs such as a ridge tent tend to be cheaper because cutting out and stitching is simple. The moment variations are introduced, such as bell ends, slopes and tapers, up goes the price. Whatever fabric is used it has weight and cost so the manufacturers try to use as little as possible to enclose a usable space. A hemisphere gives maximum volume for minimum surface area but is difficult to construct and is therefore expensive. Tents of this shape are likely to be more popular in future as technology improves.

An American geodesic-vector-
equilibrium two-skin tent

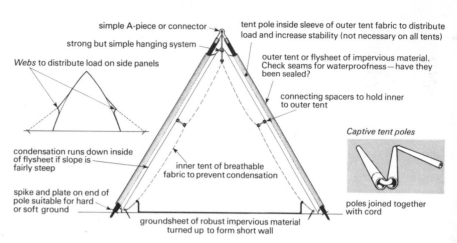

simple A-piece or connector

tent pole inside sleeve of outer tent fabric to distribute load and increase stability (not necessary on all tents)

strong but simple hanging system

Webs to distribute load on side panels

outer tent or flysheet of impervious material. Check seams for waterproofness—have they been sealed?

connecting spacers to hold inner to outer tent

Captive tent poles

condensation runs down inside of flysheet if slope is fairly steep

inner tent of breathable fabric to prevent condensation

spike and plate on end of pole suitable for hard or soft ground

poles joined together with cord

groundsheet of robust impervious material turned up to form short wall

Basic design features of a modern backpacker's tent

First and foremost, your tent should not weigh more than 4lb per person capacity. Other requirements are that it should be easy to pitch in strong winds and rain, in darkness, and when your hands are cold and you are very tired. Many modern tents have become too gimmicky in an effort to save weight and are full of small hooks, elastic bands and washers. They can be extremely difficult to pitch in bad conditions.

Normally it is best to choose a simple, uncomplicated tent with a sewn-in groundsheet to keep out draughts, sand, insects and snow. Ideally it should be one where you can hang the inner tent under the impervious down-to-earth flysheet or outer tent. This is a great help when striking camp in wet weather as everything can be packed into the rucksack under cover except the flysheet. At the last moment this can then be taken down, shaken to rid it of most of the water (= weight) and placed in the top of the rucksack ready to be dried at the first opportunity during the day, say at the lunch break.

Every tent should have reasonable storage space under the flysheet or outer tent for keeping boots, rucksacks, wet clothes and maybe for cooking in extreme weather. Choose a tent fabric which is fire retardant (see photograph of burning tent on p. 16). Most tents are made either of proofed cotton, or of various types of nylon such as ripstop which in turn may be proofed with a variety of chemicals such as polyurethane or silicone (see Appendix for details).

The latter impervious materials suffer badly from condensation

49

and adequate ventilation needs to be provided if this is not to become a problem. Ventilators, adjustable gaps, or panels of breathable material (such as Gore-Tex, see below) are usually incorporated to overcome this problem. Alternatively, the slope of the impervious flysheet should be steep enough to ensure that the droplets of condensation run down the inside to the ground without wetting the inner tent. Spacers and centre panel guy ropes are often used to ensure that this happens.

Single-skin tents These are being developed by a number of manufacturers to save weight and for their simplicity. They have been used in America for some years and are based on the new 'wonder' laminated fabrics such as 'Gore-Tex' which 'breathe' to prevent condensation on the inside but still remain completely rainproof (see Appendix). Guard against some single-skin tents which work well provided that nothing is touching the fabric during rainfall – they suffer from a contact-leak phenomenon.

Many of these latest tent designs have glass-fibre rods to support the fabric. Before purchase test these by bending them fairly hard and check at the same time for glass fibre splinters by running your fingers carefully over the stressed rod. Good ones will not splinter.

Tent accessories Most tents use thick rubber guy-rings or shock cords together with a variety of pegs and guy ropes to hold the tent in place (see illustrations). Much depends on the type of terrain as to which pegs are most suitable. Large ones work best in soft ground, such as soil, sand and snow, but smaller chrome-moly steel pegs are good for rocky ground. On the whole, the bigger the peg the greater the weight. With ingenuity most tents can be pitched without pegs (see pp. 15-22 on bivouacking).

Stones can be used to help anchor tent pegs; drive pegs in at an angle of 90° to the guy-line if you can (left) A rubber guy or 'shock-cord' in use (right)

Tent care Never store your tent away for long in a damp or wet condition. Even on a journey try to dry it out whenever possible. Canvas will mildew and go musty if left wet, and so will nylon, to a lesser extent (see Appendix). Maintain your tent in good condition. Carry a small repair kit, available at most outdoor shops, to mend small tears, broken guys or punctured groundsheets. If pitching on sharp stony ground or spiky vegetation, place a thin sheet of expanded polyurethane under the tent to protect the groundsheet. Keep the groundsheet as clean as possible and do not put a heated stove on it. Many backpackers carry a piece of sponge to mop up any wetness in the tent which inevitably occurs during long spells of wet weather.

Finally, it is a good idea to pitch your tent at home before going off on a long trip, just to make sure you have enough pegs, poles, spacers etc., and that your 'fabric house' is in good repair.

Sleeping bags

There is no such thing as an ideal sleeping bag. It all depends on what you want it for – sleeping in a tent in summer or sleeping out in the open in winter. The same bag will not fulfil both requirements. You would be either too hot or too cold in one situation or the other. The best answer is to buy two bags. First obtain a lightweight summer bag (a one-season bag). There are some good fibre pile bags of this kind on the market which are excellent and not too expensive. They are a good way to get started into summer bivouacking and camping.

Later, or if you want to sleep out say in the spring and autumn, a medium-weight bag would be a good buy. This way you get three choices of insulation, both bags together in winter and the others according to temperature. Make sure the outer bag is larger than the inner one. If the temperature gets really cold wear some clothes as well.

The purpose of the sleeping bag is to trap a layer of still air round your body to enable you to keep warm whilst asleep. The efficiency with which it does that depends on a number of variables such as the basic overall shape, the type of construction and the filling material (see Appendix). Other design features in relation to keeping the head and feet warm should be considered. (See diagrams on p. 53.) It is not much use having an expensive down filling in a badly-designed bag or a well-designed bag and poor filling. Naturally the better the design and the better the filling the more expensive the bag will be. Some expedition-type sleeping bags cost more than £100. In the end it has to be a compromise between what you need (different from what you want) and what you can afford. The two-bag system helps in this respect.

A variety of filling materials are used to create the layer of still air. Traditionally, down feathers have been used for this purpose and weight for weight there is no doubt that they are the best in dry conditions. However, world demand has outstripped supply and they are prohibitively expensive. Manufacturers have tried to overcome the problem by mixing down with various kinds of feathers which are cheaper. Sometimes even these mixes prove too costly for ordinary use and attempts have been made to find alternative fillings – mostly man-made fibres such as Terylene, and a variety of polyesters (P3, Fibrefil, Hollofil) (see Appendix).

The efficiency of the filling material depends largely on its ability to 'loft', that is to expand and fill the chamber in which it is contained. Most sleeping bags are given a 'Tog' value (see p. 54), which is a way of expressing its thermal insulation properties. However, these values should not be taken too seriously as the insulation properties of any filling go down in relation to factors such as compression and humidity. Down is the least effective in wet conditions and its insulation value when compressed (under pressure points such as the hip and shoulder) is reduced by 90 per cent. Man-made fillings which are not as good as natural duck down in dry conditions certainly score better in wet or damp atmospheres. Under compression they lose about 70 per cent of their insulation. Sleeping bags are best stored unpacked when not in use to prevent permanent compression of the filling. Hanging them on a coat hanger is best. A 'Togometer' in the Textile Department at Leeds University is being used in a research project to learn more about the properties of filling materials. As well as a sleeping bag, some kind of sleeping mat is essential to insulate the body from the cold ground. Various closed cell foam mats are on the market for this purpose together with 'self-inflating' Lilos. This is a lightweight version of a Lilo filled with foam which prevents the air circulating inside. When not in use the air can be squeezed out and the hole plugged. When required for use the plug is removed and the foam expands to fill the bed with air again.

Sleeping bags – basic shapes and construction methods

Other design features

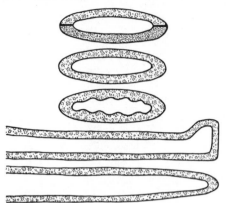

Side baffles. Some bags have different fillings, down on top and less compressible man-made fibre on bottom.

Differential cut. The outer layer of fabric is made larger than the inner layer, allowing the filling to 'loft' as much as possible. It also prevents cold spots at knees and elbows.

Space filler cut. Inner and outer layers of fabric cut the same sizes, allowing the more floppy inner layer to mould round the body.

Box foot. Gives feet more room to move and greater insulation. Warmer than simple foot.

Simple foot. Not as warm as box foot, but cheaper.

Basic shapes

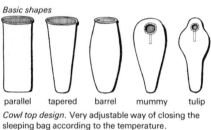

parallel   tapered   barrel   mummy   tulip

Cowl top design. Very adjustable way of closing the sleeping bag according to the temperature.

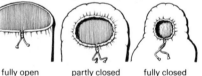

fully open   partly closed   fully closed

Construction
Sections through wall of bag show how filling is kept in place

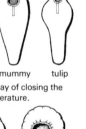

Simple quilting. Heat is lost where the stitching passes through the fabric

Double quilting. Effectively, two simple quilts fastened together in an off-set way to eliminate cold spots. Double the material so tends to be heavy.

Box wall. Prevents the filling from moving about without becoming as heavy as double quilting.

Slant wall. Prevents down from moving about but gives it room to expand.

Overlapping tube or *V-baffle.* Very efficient but heavy because it uses a lot of material.

A consideration of sleeping bags would not be complete without mentioning fibre pile. It is used widely as insulating clothing and has been employed in a range of sleeping bags. One of its main advantages is that it does not compress like traditional filled sleeping bags. An insulating mat, therefore, is less important. Different thicknesses of pile are used for summer only, spring/autumn and winter bags, and these can be used together. The summer bag makes an excellent liner or inner bag to supplement an old or medium-weight bag in winter. The principal property of fibre pile is its very good performance when wet. If completely soaked and then wrung out it still provides satisfactory insulation and ensures a good night's sleep. Other attributes are that it can easily be put in the washer and subsequently dried out.

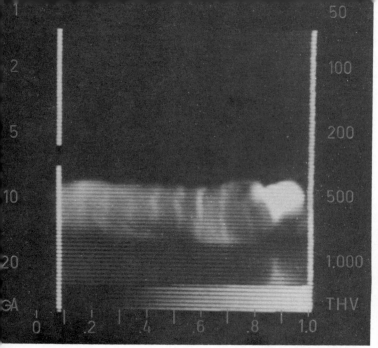

Thermograph picture shows heat escaping from stitching line of sleeping bag (white areas)

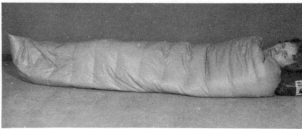

The sleeping bag in the Thermograph picture

Fibre pile works best when in close contact with the body and for this reason the sleeping bags are mostly tulip-shaped.

Tog value

The method by which we measure the insulating power of a textile fabric is to measure the drop in temperature across the thickness of a sample which is in contact with an electrically heated plate. The amount by which a fabric resists the transfer of heat from the plate can be measured and from this a Tog value can be assigned.

$$\text{'10 Togs'} = \frac{\text{temperature difference across the sample}}{\text{Watts per (metre)}^2 \ W/M^2}$$

Rucksacks and load carrying

Man, a vertical skeletal structure walking on two legs, is not well-designed as a pack animal. Since he walked the earth he has been faced with the problem of carrying his essential needs of food and water. In early times killing a large animal was one thing, carrying it back home was another. Carrying water, very heavy stuff, has always been a problem to him especially in dry and desert regions. The age-old quest of how best to carry our requirements on foot is still as pertinent to today's backpacker as it was to early man. Some ethnic groups, notably the Sherpas of Nepal, are famous for their ability to carry heavy loads, often spurning the technologically designed ergonomic expedition rucksack in favour of their traditional method using a tump-band (a band by which some of the weight is transferred to the forehead). Other groups such as eastern women, African porters, and Smithfield market men traditionally carry quite heavy loads balanced on top of their heads.

Man has discovered by experience that the best way to carry a heavy weight is to get it as near as possible to his centre of gravity, which for the majority of people is in the middle of the body at about the level of the navel. Women instinctively carry heavy children on one hip for this reason. Many modern rucksacks have hip-belts for the same reason (see also p. 56). The next best position is to get the weight *over* the centre of gravity like the African porter and the eastern waterpot carriers. Carrying a heavy weight a long way from the centre of gravity, for instance in one hand, is very strenuous and tiring due to the increased muscular activity required for maintaining balance.

Modern backpacker-type rucksacks are designed to meet these principles of load-carrying by keeping the weight close to the back and fairly high up, so that by leaning slightly forwards the weight is brought over the centre of gravity with the least muscular effort. It also enables the backpacker to stand reasonably erect and in balance. The actual weight can either be hung on the shoulders or be made to rest on the hips by means of a hip-belt, or a combination of both. Much depends on your own personal anatomy: broad-shouldered, slender-hipped people are more suited to, and often prefer to, take most of the weight on their shoulders; conversely, narrow shouldered, shapely-hipped people prefer and are suited to take most of the weight on their hips via a hip-belt. Many modern rucksacks are designed to do either one or the other or both, depending on how the straps are adjusted.

Traditionally the weight has been taken on the shoulders with the weight up high – the so-called 'high-pack' method. This has meant tired aching shoulders almost as an inevitable part of backpacking. In modern times broad, foam-padded shoulder straps have increased the comfort level by cushioning and spreading the load but have not removed the ache due to sheer weight alone. Some people, often girls, suffer from numbness in the arms known as the 'shopping-bag syndrome', which is caused by stretching of the nerves in the neck and shoulders (brachial plexus) as a result of carrying shoulder-hung rucksacks. The spine also comes in for quite a lot of compression in this method, occasionally giving rise to backache. Nevertheless many people prefer to take the weight on their shoulders. A lot depends on the magnitude of the load.

The hip-belt has become popular in recent times because it takes the weight off the shoulders on to the hips (the pelvis). The strong, rigid pelvis transfers the weight directly to the legs through the hip joint which in turn is supported by the very powerful thigh and leg muscles. It alleviates cramping of the chest, making breathing easier,

Rucksack hip belts: swivel (left) and fixed (right)

Frameless rucksack

and does not stress the shoulders and spine; at the same time it brings the load close to the centre of gravity. It makes for stability and comfort. When wearing a properly fitting hip-belt-type rucksack it should be possible to put your thumbs under the shoulder straps with ease, thus demonstrating that little if any weight is being taken by the shoulders. The main disadvantage of the hip-belt sometimes occurs in very hot humid weather, especially if you are walking several hours day after day. The hips can become very sore indeed with the heat and sweat which is difficult to avoid under a broad, close-fitting harness.

As with most other backpacking equipment there is a bewildering selection of rucksacks available. Make sure the one you choose *fits* you and is suitable for what you want to do. In the shop load it with a significant amount of gear, say 40lb weight, and wear it for half an hour. Better still, borrow one like it from a friend, load it with plenty of gear (not foam plastic) and take a ten-mile walk. If it feels comfortable then you know it is safe to buy.

The manufacturers overcome the 'fit' or size problem either by making a range of sizes or by producing adjustable frames combined with a range of 'sack' shapes. They fall into three main types: frameless, external frames and internal frames.

Frameless packs

These have certain advantages over framed ones insofar as they are lighter, roll up and pack away when empty and make good contact with the back, which improves stability. The only disadvantage here is a sweaty back and the possibility of something hard protruding if not packed well. Many are high enough to be efficient – notably the Outward Bound type – and several have hip-belts attached. Some manufacturers have a system of packs and frames which can be used separately or together, giving thirty combinations. This makes it possible to buy a frameless 'sack' to begin with and then later, when you can afford it, buy a frame to match it. This gives you more flexibility as well.

*External-frame rucksacks
(pack frames)*

The idea is not new. Pack frames made of wood have been used by Indians and trappers in the Yukon for a very long time, long before aluminium and nylon were invented. However, modern technology has improved on an old idea with light aluminium alloy tubes and

External-frame rucksack, with a pocket modification for easy stowage of woolly hat, gloves etc., without removing the rucksack

plastics. The emphasis has been on high packs with frames shaped to match the curvature of the spine, bringing the weight close to the centre of gravity. Some are welded together in a range of sizes; others are fastened together with screws or pins, making them adjustable. On some it is possible to fit an extension to make them taller. Make sure you buy one that fits or can be made to fit you. (Adjustable ones can be used by different members of the family at different times.)

Mostly these are H- or ladder-shaped with curved horizontal members to clear the spine. Back-bands made of mesh or nylon pulled taut by lacing or turnbuckle screws rest against the back. This design has the advantage of providing ventilation for the back. Very heavy weights have been carried on rigid pack frames. 'Sacks' designed to fit them tend to be more versatile than other types, often having lots of pockets and compartments. Extra items and awkward shapes can be accommodated easily on a pack frame – the danger is that you will carry too much. Most can be bought with a hip-belt. The floating type (see p. 56) is best suited to a pack frame.

The main disadvantages are that external-frame rucksacks are awkward to use in confined spaces such as a tent and catch on branches and rocks in tight places, though they do make good supports when bivouacking. Car owners fear damage to their cars on seeing a pack frame. When not in use they can present a storage problem.

Internal-frame packs

Some simple 'sacks' have an inverted U-shaped alloy tube sandwiched inside the material to give support and rigidity to an otherwise uncomplicated bag. Most internal-framed rucksacks, however, are much more sophisicated than this and are known as 'anatomic' or 'ergonomic' rucksacks. The aim of the design is, as usual, to keep the weight close to the back whilst at the same time transferring the loading onto the hips by using an integral hip-belt. The frames, which provide some rigidity, come in fixed, malleable or adjustable form to accommodate the contours of the wearer. Many are padded or ribbed to overcome the 'sweaty back' problem. Most tend to be smaller than high pack frames but are more stable as all lateral movement is eliminated. The performance of this type of rucksack is very dependent on it being the correct size and fitting. Make sure the hip-belt has a quick-release buckle in case of emergency.

General notes on rucksacks

The volume or carrying capacity of rucksacks is given in litres. It is interesting to note that most other items such as packed sleeping bags are given in inches (e.g., 16" x 8" diameter). It would be helpful if there was a standard measure of volume. A rucksack of 55 litres capacity is about normal for the average backpacker.

Not surprisingly, they are made in a wide range of fabrics (see Appendix). Cotton duck tends to hold water, gets heavier, freezes and will rot in time but it is hard wearing, 'breathes' and keeps its shape well. On the other hand P.U.-coated Nylon is light, strong and water-repellent but is not so hard-wearing. The proofed coatings are easily abraded. No rucksack is weatherproof in conditions of driving rain, Scotch mist or spindrift (powdered snow). Seams should be sealed and a polythene bag liner used to protect the contents. A poncho-type cape with a 'blister' on the back will protect both walker and rucksack. Elasticated rucksack covers are also available to keep out the bad weather.

A number of secondary design features need to be considered when buying a rucksack. Personal preference is the only criterion when it comes to deciding on how many and where pockets should be, whether or not to have any compartments in the rucksack, whether these should be horizontal or vertical. Each have their merits in terms of packing and access. Most backpackers prefer compartments and lots of pockets, which make it much easier to organise one's gear and find things, especially small items such as maps, first aid, food and waterproofs.

Rucksacks old and new!

Other points to look for are quick-release toggles on the draw cord, elasticated flaps to keep out the weather and prevent loss of small items, buckles that can be opened and closed with mitts on and buckle straps that are captive and never need re-threading.

Packing the rucksack

Your rucksack load should equal about a quarter of your body weight if you are to enjoy backpacking. Certainly it should not exceed one-third of your weight unless you are on an extended expedition of some kind. Because of necessary extra equipment winter loads tend to be somewhat heavy. Carrying too much can be counter-productive. Weigh your packed rucksack before starting out.

Actual packing is largely common sense. Put heavy items near the back, avoiding protrusions. Keep items needed on the journey and on arrival fairly accessible. Wrap sleeping bag and dry clothes in separate polythene bags. The sleeping mat can be rolled up and carried either above or below the sack on the outside. Alternatively some people make it into a large cylinder and use it as a sack liner. This is a good idea in bad weather. Rolled-up sleeping mats often blow away in strong winds. Stove fuel is best carried in an outside pocket in case of leakage, and is handy there for a midday brew.

Putting the loaded rucksack on

To avoid straining your back keep it straight at all times. If possible lift the rucksack on to a bench, wall or similar, back up to it and thread your arms through the straps. Otherwise first hoist it on to your thigh, thread one arm through a strap and shunt it round on to your back.

Stoves

For practical and ecological reasons small camp fires are becoming a thing of the past, except near a lake, river or sea beach where drift-wood is often readily available. It is still great fun and extremely satisfying to cook on an open fire. A small gridiron is a useful asset on which to rest your pans. Beware of exploding stones as the water soaked inside converts to steam. Nowadays there is a whole range of portable stoves suitable for backpacking which are quicker and more versatile than lighting fires.

Before choosing a stove you have to decide what type of activity you have in mind and how much you can afford. Inevitably, like most things in backpacking, it is a compromise, and depends much on your personal requirements. Availability of the basic fuel in remote areas, weight and capital cost (you can pay from 90p to £35), as well as where and when you plan to use it, will also influence your choice of stove. If you are wise you will check the manufacturer's specifications in relation to weight and efficiency. Virtually all manufacturers make some claim that their particular model of stove will boil a measured amount of water in a given number of minutes. None, so far as I am aware, give any factual data. None give the starting temperature of the water, or the conditions under which the test was held, nor do they say at what point the clock was started. Was it when the first match was struck? Does it include assembly and/or pre-heating time where applicable?

There are three basic forms of fuel: solids, liquids and gases. In theory the more volatile the fuel the more efficiently it burns. However, in practice much depends on the design and efficiency of the stove itself and from a backpacking point of view there are other important considerations such as weight, cost, stability and potential dangers.

In the spring of 1978, at the University of Leeds, a physics lecturer ran an experimental pilot scheme to evaluate a variety of back-packers' stoves. The temperature of the assembled stove containing fuel was reduced to 0°C. An accurately measured ½ litre of water at 0.5°C was placed on the stove which was immediately lit. The time to boiling point was then measured together with the amount of fuel used. Unfortunately some of the stoves were not consistent per-formers and different stoves of the same model perform differently so the results can only be used as a guide. (All measurements in this section are given in grammes and litres to make comparison easier.)

In the solid fuel range the *Kari Cooker* burning large Hexamine fuel tablets is the most significant. It is widely used by young people of limited means. It is very cheap to buy (about £1), is very lightweight (106gms) and the fuel is efficient, safe and easy to use. The stove and the fuel are almost indestructible and foolproof. On test it was the most efficient stove tested in terms of times to raise water from 0°C to boiling point – 3 to 4½ minutes – using only one tablet of fuel (weight 28gms). Being much wider than it is tall it makes for a stable, safe stove. The main drawback is that you cannot regulate the heat in any way and the tablets are very difficult to extinguish (an asset on occasions). It is an ideal beginner's stove.

Apart from the proverbial 'Tommy Cooker' of war-time fame, which used a jelly type of fuel in a tin and is almost obsolete now, the only other solid fuel cooker available is the *Esbit*. This is exactly the same design as the Kari Cooker but smaller; it burns Metaldehyde tablets which are sometimes marketed for killing garden slugs but more often as primer fuel for starting paraffin stoves. It has the same characteristics as the Kari Cooker, but weighs only 86gms, and is not suitable for anything but a small pan. Seven 'Meta' fuel tablets (equivalent in weight to one Kari Cooker tablet) were used to raise ½ litre of water at 0°C to boiling point in 6½ minutes.

Liquid fuels for backpacking stoves in Britain are paraffin, petrol and methylated spirit. The safest of these by far is paraffin. 'Primus'-type stoves have been with us a long time and have proved their worth beyond doubt. One of the most popular backpacking stoves in this class is the *Optimus 96L* which weighs 794gms and has a 284ml capacity. It is housed in pieces in a small tin box which fits into the pocket of most rucksacks. When required for use it has to be assembled (there are thirteen moveable pieces), which in bad conditions can be troublesome. Also the loss of any one piece is likely to inactivate the stove. The box contains a separate pricker and a spanner. It requires a lot of care and maintenance. The flame is controlled by carefully releasing the pressure in the tank. Its efficiency was not tested at Leeds.

A really robust, almost infallible paraffin stove for serious expedition or winter use is the *Optimus 111.* It is rather heavy at 1,588gms and currently costs £35. However, in very harsh conditions it has proved reliable and something of a life-saver. In my opinion the extra weight is worth carrying when daily hot food is imperative to one's survival. I have used one for nearly twenty years in extremes of climate up mountains, down potholes, from the heat of the desert to the cold of a snow hole. Normal maintenance ensures unfailing service. It is ready assembled in a square box with a drop front. Almost every part is fixed and cannot easily be lost. It has an inbuilt pricker for cleaning the jet at the turn of a handle and the flame can be regulated from a full roar to a small simmer-type flame with the same handle without losing pressure in the tank. It is very stable as the box is an integral part of the stove. The lid also serves as an additional windbreak and reflects some heat from the burner – a quality which can be enhanced with a piece of kitchen aluminium foil. The tank holds 568ml of paraffin.

One of the disadvantages of all paraffin stoves is that they need a primer fuel such as methylated spirit, 'Meta' fuel tablets, or Optimus burning paste to get them going. I have a preference for the 'Meta' tablets as they are much more durable than the other two. Whilst it does not do the stove any good, knowledgeable campers can light a paraffin stove without a primer fuel. In the Leeds test it took several minutes to get the stove going from freezing point but then it boiled the $\frac{1}{2}$ litre of water from 0°C in five minutes.

Petrol stoves are well liked by some people. They are quite efficient and do not require a primer fuel to get them going. A small quantity of petrol is encouraged to flow through the jet and into the ring cup which is then used to pre-heat the stove. The main drawback with petrol stoves is the highly volatile nature of the fuel itself. Every precaution should be taken to prevent leaks. The petrol vapour itself is heavy and tends to creep along the ground. It has a relatively low flash point and any spark or naked flame is likely to cause an explosion. Spare petrol should be stored in a leak-proof metal container and labelled 'Petroleum spirit – highly inflammable' (this is required by law). One of the main advantages is that petrol is universally available and whilst it says on many new petrol stoves 'use only un-leaded petrol', they work quite well on the lowest grade of petrol at the pumps. A small thumb-operated pump with tubing is available to enable you to fill your stove from a car fuel tank, if you are really stuck, garages are shut – and you can find a willing car owner!

Probably the most popular petrol stove is the *Svea 123* which is an integrated design of stove, windshield and cooking pot. It weighs 505gms and holds 190ml of petrol. In the Leeds test it took eleven minutes to boil a $\frac{1}{2}$ litre of water from 0°C. It is ideal for one-person cooking. The flame can be controlled by turning a key-style handle at the side. Other good petrol stoves are the *88N* and the more stable *99* which is a box shape, the square lid serving as a pan, though the more recent *Optimus 323* is a superior design. The heaviest and most powerful is the *111B* which is the twin of the paraffin stove *111*. It has all the same advantages. If you go abroad make sure you know the correct words for the fuel. In some countries petrol means paraffin.

Methylated spirit is the other remaining liquid fuel. This is somewhat safer than petrol but not as safe as paraffin. It is very difficult to see the flame in sunshine and any spilt 'meths' which becomes ignited creeps invisibly along, maybe causing a fire some distance from the spillage. Meths is a nice clean fuel compared to paraffin and petrol, the smell of which is difficult to eradicate, especially from food. A picnic stove costing less than £1 and weighing only 230gms is an ideal beginner's stove. Obviously it has limitations at that price but it is quite adequate for overnight stops in summer and for cooking uncomplicated meals. In the Leeds test it took twelve minutes to boil $\frac{1}{2}$ litre of water from 0°C.

Two sophisticated meths stoves where the burner, windshield and pans are incorporated in the design are currently available. They are very similar: one is the *Trangia* from Karrimor and the other is the *Optimus 77A*, somewhat lighter at 756gms. Both are stable and efficiently designed and tend to work better in a breeze, hence their classification as 'storm cookers'. An additional ring dropped over the burner provides a 'simmer' flame. There is no fine adjustment. In the Leeds test the 77A took ten minutes to boil ½ litre of water from 0°C. This was in still air. Methylated spirit is the most expensive liquid fuel and is not readily available in remote areas: these are the main disadvantages.

Liquified Petroleum Gas (LPG) stoves are now beginning to take an ever-increasing share of the backpackers' stove market. Intensive competition between the major companies is working to the advantage of the customer. Lower prices and newer and better designs are currently being developed. The LPG in this context is nearly always butane with a boiling point of −11.5°C. On the whole these butane gas stoves do not work well at low temperatures. The *Vango ALP 8100 All Weather Stove* is the exception at the moment. It has a loop near the burner which vaporises the liquid gas, enabling it to be used even at low temperatures. It accepts a variety of self-sealing cans of gas, including the Calor Primus 2202 can specially developed for the 1975 British Everest Expedition. The *Vango ALP 7000* stove, which sits on the ground and connects to a variety of self-sealing cans by means of a short length of tubing, is also worthy of note. It is amazingly compact and safe.

Originally all LPG stoves worked by screwing down a spike to puncture the can so the gas could pass up into the burner. In cold weather when the stove was not working well many people, thinking the cylinder was empty, unscrewed the appliance, allowing the dangerous LPG gas to escape. There are still a few of this type about. For your own sake, only purchase burners which fit on to self-sealing disposable butane cans. Choose a design which is squat and

The Vango ALP 8100 gas stove

stable. Many of the earlier models were too tall in relation to the size of their base.

All stoves, with the exception of the Optimus 77A and Trangia meths stoves, need complete protection from the wind if they are to work efficiently. Even a slight air movement will take a great deal of heat away from your cooking pot. It is essential to get your stove out of the wind by forming some kind of wind break. Find a sheltered place if possible, otherwise use a wind shield, or use stones, people or rucksacks to keep the wind off your stove.

Think twice about taking a stove into your tent, and avoid it wherever possible. Obviously when you are very familiar with your stove, and hopefully you understand it fully, the risk of using it in the tent is minimal. In very bad weather it is sometimes the only way. Make sure the stove is stable, preferably on a flat stone. If there are two of you in the tent it is often a good plan if only one does the cooking. This way the risk of an accidental fire is reduced. Take all possible care: every year a number of tents burn down within a few seconds.

Carrying liquid fuels

An unorthodox way of carrying stove fuel

Liquid fuels, especially petrol and methylated spirit, should be carried in lightweight aluminium bottles with leak-proof screwed stoppers. These are usually available in outdoor equipment shops. On no account should petrol or meths be carried in polythene containers. These highly volatile fuels permeate through the plastic and become dangerous near a naked flame or spark. Paraffin on the other hand may be carried quite safely in leak-proof polythene bottles designed for the purpose. They have the advantage that you can observe the fuel when pouring and can see how much fuel you have left. Normally it is wise to carry your spare fuel in an outside pocket of your rucksack where it is readily available and where, if it leaks, it is less likely to contaminate your food and equipment.

A novel idea you might try if you have have an all-welded aluminium tubular pack frame is to fill the hollow tubes with fuel. Obviously you have to blank off the bottom of the tube and arrange a tap or removable plug at the top end for pouring out the contents. One make of pack frame currently on the market holds just over 284ml of liquid in each of the side tubes and is easily converted into a spare fuel tank.

Checklists of equipment

	at first:	add later:	optional extras:
Summer valley stroll	small rucksack waterproofs small first aid kit map(s) and compass	stove pans or billies fuel matches mug, spoon, knife, tin-opener, fork food	sunglasses camera water bottle

Summer bivouac	large rucksack
	plastic sheeting
	  (heavy gauge)
	nylon string (plenty)
	small repair kit
	large polythene
	  survival bag
	sleeping bag
	insulating mat
	stove
	billies
	fuel (+ extra)
		spoon, knife, fork
		  tin-opener
		water bottle
		food
		plastic scourer,
		  J-cloth
		torch
		first aid kit
		watch
		map(s)
		compass
		whistle
			Balaclava
			mitts
			waterproof cagoule
			  and over-trousers
			strong footwear
			breeches or long
			  trousers (*not* jeans)
			other personal
			  clothing

Summer camping add the following to the list for summer bivouacking: tent (check poles and pegs)			

Winter activities
 	
N.B. tent (if used)
should have sewn-in
groundsheet and,
preferably, a snow
valance
	add the following to
	the list for summer
	bivouacking:
	gaiters
	heavy boots
	crampons
	ice-axe
		sun-glasses/goggles
		extra sweaters
		windproof anorak
		spare hat
		at least 2 pairs
		  spare socks
		thick trousers or
			breeches
			long johns
			outer mitts
			thick wool mitts
			spare torch batteries
			rope (120'/9mm
			  nylon)

Suggested first aid kit	selection of strip
	  plasters
	shell dressings (e.g.
	  Melolin gauze
	  squares, wound
	  dressings)
	2″ crêpe bandage
		antiseptic cream
		scissors
		small plastic bags (for
		  written messages)
		personal toiletries
		toilet paper
		tweezers
			needle
			aspirin/Paracetamol
			insect repellent
			lip salve
			sun cream
			paper
			pencil

6 Personal clothing

Well dressed winter walkers

Clothing

The function of clothing fundamentally is to protect man from the environment and to help him keep his temperature normal by creating an artificial micro-climate round him. He cannot control nature's climate but with the right kind of clothing he can control his own.

Hot weather poses problems for man (see pp. 87-88) and clothing is usually used to protect him from too much heat absorption and the burning effects of the sun. However, for most backpackers in temperate zones the problem is one of how to keep warm and dry in wind, rain and cold. The answer is to have clothing which is infinitely variable and adjustable to meet the equally variable conditions of resting and exercising in a wide range of climates.

Basically, clothing must provide insulation from the cold. It does this by trapping air, one of the best insulators, amongst its fibres. The necessary thickness of this insulating layer depends on the person, the level of activity and the environmental temperature. During exercise less insulation is required than during rest. The Appendix on Fibres and Fabrics will give you a good idea of the best kind of materials for this insulating layer (pp. 108-114).

Nearly all insulating materials lose their efficiency when wet (pile fabrics and wool are least badly affected) and must therefore be protected from the rain. The only way to do this is to cover the insulation garments with an impervious 'shell'. 'Shell clothing' in the form of anoraks, cagoules and overtrousers is readily available in the shops in a bewildering range of styles and fabrics. The Appendix should help you make a good buy.

Wearing impervious windproof and waterproof clothing during exercise causes sweat to condense on the inside of the garment and can, during prolonged activity, wet the insulating layers underneath. However, being wetted by a pint of your own warm sweat is better

Insulating layers

woolly hat (Balaclava)

wool shirt, Damart vest,
wool sweaters,
pile fibre jacket etc.

long johns made of wool,
Damart, pile fibre etc.

loop-stitched wool socks
(1 or 2 pairs)

Shell clothing

wire hood or vizor

draw-cord to close hood in bad weather

impervious anorak

waist draw cord (to trap warm air)

double-ended zip for versatile ventilation

cuffs wide enough to ventilate; Velcro
fasteners to close when necessary

long sleeves to protect hands from wind
and rain

overtrousers with zip up to knee for easy
dressing, and long enough to fit over
footwear

Clothing considerations:'shell
clothing' covers insulating layers

Note the wired vizor round the hood,
which is spacious enough to take a
Balaclava helmet, and the
double-ended zip with press-stud
overlap

than being irrigated by gallons of cold rainwater all day long. Fabrics
which allow moisture vapour to escape but do not let the rain in are
being developed and improved and may help to solve this problem.

In order to meet all the various circumstances you should buy
clothing which is versatile. Two thin layers are better than one thick
layer. Choose garments which are adjustable and which can be
opened and closed down the front and at the cuffs. This applies to
insulating garments as well as 'shell' clothing. Anoraks with chunky
double-ended zips are much preferable to the over-the-head,
all-on-all-off type of garment which cannot be vented whilst walking.
Cuffs should be generously cut to allow ventilation when necessary
and to fit over mitts and gloves at the wrist, and it
should be possible to seal them up in bad weather. Velcro straps are
usually best. Hoods should also be generous and designed to protect
the face in bad conditions by means of a tunnel or wired peak. Hoods
which are too small to accommodate both your head and a woolly hat
or Balaclava are no good. Pockets should be generous enough to hold
your map, compass, gloves and woolly hat readily available for use.
This saves time and makes you and your clothing more efficient.
When buying waterproof overtrousers make absolutely sure that you
will be able to get them on and off without removing your boots.

The hands, feet and face are the most difficult parts of the body to
protect in bad weather, especially in wet, cold conditions. The hands
can be protected by withdrawing them into the sleeves of the anorak –

some people sew on a sleeve extension for this purpose. On the whole, mitts are better than gloves for keeping the hands warm. Some people keep them handy in cold dry weather (and prevent losing them) by fastening them to the wrists with tape (see illustration on p. 67). Waterproof and windproof overmitts (shell clothing for the hands) are desirable in very bad conditions. Some woollen mitts are knitted oversize in unshrunken wool which is subsequently washed to shrink them down to proper size. This makes them windproof, hardwearing and very efficient insulators. Because there is a 20 per cent heat loss from the head, 'If you want to keep your feet warm, wear a hat' – the woolly hat is not just a gimmick, it really works.

Footwear

There is a great deal of confused thinking about suitable footwear for walking and backpacking. Notice that I carefully avoid using the word 'boots' as this simply pre-judges the topic.

The owner of the feet is more important than the footwear. This cannot be stressed too much. In other words, the best boot in the world is not going to make an unfit, inexperienced person a sure-footed mountaineer. It will not immediately endow him with leg strength, balance and the skills and knowledge necessary to negotiate steep and rough terrain. There is no 'magic-boot': there is *no substitute* for knowledge and training. By the same token, soft unused feet are not going to be spared blisters if they are suddenly put into a pair of 'leather prisons' and subjected to walking ten or twenty miles a day. People must accept that there are no short-cut methods. Soaking the feet in methylated spirit or some other potion may help fractionally, but really there is no successful alternative to a sensible graded walking programme to condition both feet and footwear.

Remember that millions of people all over the world do not wear any footwear at all. Many of them walk long distances over hot stony ground without discomfort. Whilst it is true that most have walked barefoot since childhood, they are only made of flesh and blood like you are. Think about that. I often visit a place about 100 miles along the Pennine Way and I have noticed that very many Pennine Wayfarers walk along in very light footwear (gym shoes, sandals etc.) with their boots tied to their rucksacks, especially in summer. Engaged in conversation, they always complain that their feet become hot and blistered in their boots and that the lightweight

Winter conditions in the mountains.
Is *your* clothing good enough?

footwear brings relief and comfort. Many successfully complete the walk without boots. Therein lies a message.

Before going out to buy footwear, ask yourself why it is necessary to put something on your feet in the first place? Consider what you plan to do in this foot gear. Easy walks in easy countryside in summer can be done in almost anything. Boots are not necessary. In fact boots are often an over-rated piece of personal equipment. It all depends on what you intend to do, where and in what conditions. Obviously there is specially designed footwear for particular purposes, for example clog-dancing, ice-skating, fell running, rock climbing, skiing, winter mountaineering etc. No single type of footwear could possibly cater for more than one of these specialist activities.

Walking, which is fundamental to backpacking, is rather similar. There is such a wide variety of environments and terrain that maybe no one piece of footwear can adequately cope with them all. An insulated tough mountain boot suitable for winter use in snow and cold wet moorland bogs would almost certainly cause over-heating of the feet and blisters if used on long hot days in summer. Conversely, a light summer boot is inadequate for the rigours and cold of winter hill walking: inevitably cold wet feet would result plus the risk of cold damage to the tissues, not to mention the inability to kick steps in snow.

The footwear should protect the feet from the environment to a greater or lesser degree – much depends on the skill and knowledge of the walker. A competent person can travel safely over the hills in poor footwear if he wants to, because he will pick the most appropriate route to suit his footwear. Also he will be very skilful in knowing how and where to place his feet, whereas the novice will not

A variety of heavy and lightweight footwear for backpacking. Note padded ankles and different tread patterns

be able to do that and will probably come to grief. Remember it is not the footwear but the person in them that counts.

The feet should be protected from physical damage caused by rocks, stones, sand, soil, harsh vegetation such as brambles, thorns, bushes, nettles etc., and from extremes of temperature, both of heat and cold. Water, mud and snow are variable factors in relation to foot temperature. The footwear should provide a reasonably stable platform for the foot to rest on and distribute the point loading from rocks and stones to the whole foot. Finally, it needs a suitable non-slip sole underneath which is appropriate for the terrain to be crossed. Naturally the footwear needs to be a comfortable fit and easy to put on and take off, which means an efficient method of lacing.

A huge misconception exists amongst many experienced walkers which is worth mentioning here. It is that a boot must support the ankle to give it strength. The truth is that a well-supported ankle will become weaker in time and will be more likely to get sprained than an unsupported ankle. Weak ankles need exercising to strengthen them, not supporting – ask any physiotherapist. The outcome of this misconception is that many people buy boots which are very stiff round the ankles and often too high. Such boots regularly cause severe pain and chafing above the ankle bones and not infrequently damage the Achilles tendon at the back. Walking becomes very painful, if not impossible, when this happens and tendons take a long time to repair. The point to understand is that the ankle bones need protection from abrasion and impact, *not* support. There are now plenty of types of footwear on the market which do just that.

Choosing footwear, like most things, is a compromise between requirements (that is job specification) and cost. You normally get what you pay for. You do not need an expensive boot unless you are going to do something ambitious or operate in winter conditions. You should be able to find something suitable at an ordinary shoe shop, a store like the Army and Navy Stores, or a farm supplier. More sophisticated footwear (therefore more expensive) is sold in specialist outdoor shops. For walking generally you need a flexible sole. Steer clear of rigid-soled boots unless you want to get involved in a bit of mountaineering: this type of boot has a propensity for generating blisters at the back of your heel. Consider the weight of the boot. Remember that one pound carried on the foot is equal in energy terms to five pounds carried on the back. That is a very significant fact on a twenty-mile walk. Most people like to keep their feet dry so consider something with a bellows tongue to keep out the water. Wet feet do not cause bad colds (another myth).

Something to put on the feet comes in all shapes, sizes, prices and permutations of construction, leathers, fabrics and designs from lightweight training shoes to heavy mountain boots (see illustration on p. 70). The recently developed Klets Winit ecological footwear deserves special mention. Apart from the advice already given, the best idea is to visit some reputable outdoor shops, have a good look at the wide range of footwear, tell the sales person what it is you have in mind to do and trust his advice.

Make sure what you buy is a good fit. Take one or two pairs of socks with you and wear these to try on the footwear. Lace them up and walk round the shop a few times. Your toes should not touch the end, you will suffer incredible pain walking down hill if they do. They should not be too tight. Your feet will expand when warm with walking and tend to spread out when you are carrying extra weight on your back. Take plenty of time choosing – it's normal, most people do. When you get back home wear them round the house for a few hours. If they are not comfortable most reputable shops will take them back provided they have not been worn outside. It is worth going to a lot of trouble to get a good fit. Your footwear is the foundation of backpacking.

Breaking-in new boots   Lightweight boots need little if any breaking-in. Heavy kinds should be broken in gradually. Wear them round the house and garden for a few hours or go to work in them a few times. Try them out a few miles at a time to begin with, guard against blisters. New boots have a tendency to break one's feet in rather than vice-versa. When you purchase the boots find out what the recommended dressing for them is and use it. This often helps to soften the leather. There are some good proprietary brands on the market such as Suppletex, Mars Oil, Nikwax, and Kiwi Wet Proof, as well as some good silicone sprays, which all help to soften as well as preserve the leather. Before your first outdoor wearing treat the boots with a leather preservative. Eventually the boots should adapt to the shape of your feet. Wearing them in wet weather often accelerates this process.

Care of boots   Normally your boots will last a long time and give good service if you look after them. Never, ever, dry out leather footwear in front of a fire or by radiated heat from a stove. This form of heat will dry out the leather unevenly, causing cracking or in severe cases disintegration. After use, especially in moorland boggy areas, wash and brush off all traces of soil and mud and let the boots dry out naturally in a well-ventilated place. Apply some leather preservative at regular intervals.

Socks   Outer footwear, socks and feet need to be considered as an entity. Socks are almost as important as what is on the outside of your feet. They form a protective layer between the feet and the footwear. This layer has a cushioning effect as well as providing additional insulation against the cold in winter. Most people wear two pairs of socks, normally one thin pair next to the feet and a thicker outer pair. The socks should not be too tight or they will impair the blood circulation in winter. On the other hand they should not be too large or creases form inside the footwear, thus creating pain and discomfort.

All-wool socks are undoubtedly the best though nowadays many socks contain a percentage of man-made fibres to improve wear and durability. Loop-stitch socks are very popular, and when new they can be worn alone and are extremely comfortable. There is a variety of synthetic fibre socks on the market which claim to 'wick' away the perspiration from the feet. Being thin, they are often worn as an undersock in a two-sock combination.

Blisters are normally caused by local overheating due to friction or rubbing of the skin. Good socks can go a long way to eliminating this problem which can easily destroy the pleasure of a backpacking trip. Socks, like most things, need maintenance. They should be worn for one day only and then washed. This way they will last longer, retain their efficiency as an insulator and protect the feet. Dirty socks lose their insulating properties, become matted and hard and can cause blisters. On a journey at least three sets of socks are required so that at any one time a clean pair is available in the rucksack. Wash a pair daily, weather permitting, and hang them on the outside of your rucksack so they can dry whilst you are walking. Two strong safety pins – babies' nappy pins, with safety lock, are ideal – are useful for this job.

In hot weather thick socks can be a disadvantage as they cause the feet to over-heat, thus increasing the likelihood of blisters and general foot fatigue. Wear thinner socks if possible and change them in any case at frequent intervals. Hang them out on the rucksack for an airing. Remove the boots and socks and let your feet cool down during stops.

Gaiters Some backpackers like wearing gaiters most of the time except when it is hot. However, the main function of knee-length gaiters is to keep snow, mud, dirt, sand and pebbles out of the footwear, and to protect the socks from unnecessary dirt and abrasion in tough vegetation such as heather, undergrowth and brambles.

In the winter time they make a great contribution to keeping the feet warm and dry. They are made in thick canvas, proofed nylon and Gore-Tex. Usually they have a zip down the back or front with a cord passing under the instep to prevent them riding up.

Home-made gear
As you become more expert you may wish to incorporate your own ideas into your equipment, and to be able to tailor your gear to your own individual requirements is one of the great pleasures of making it yourself. With so much equipment readily available, there is no need to make anything unless you wish to, and if you do you must be very careful what fabrics and construction methods you use, to avoid disappointment. Detailed advice on all aspects of making your own gear can be obtained from the mail order firms listed on p. 115.

7 Food and catering

Breakfasting in an official high level campsite in Yosemite National Park, U.S.A.

'A sandwich in the belly is worth two in the rucksack'

Your food must fulfil four requirements – be light to carry, provide plenty of energy, be quick and easy to prepare, and be good to eat.

Lightweight food
The growth in popularity of backpacking has happened because of the development of lightweight camping gear; and food is no exception. If you go to your local camping shop you will see the wide range of lightweight food available, including separate items like vegetables, fruit, dairy products, meat or complete meals in single or double

75

portion packs. All these foods are 'dehydrated', which means that their moisture content has been removed before packing in airtight bags. This reduces the weight by up to 80 per cent and, as re-forming the food is simply a matter of mixing with a quantity of water, it makes them a great convenience for backpackers.

There are two methods of processing dehydrated foods. 'Air-dried' means the food is placed in a drum and the moisture removed by passing a stream of hot air through. The procedure is very simple, but partially destroys the actual cell structure of the food so that when reconstituted, the flavour and appearance is often rather changed. The backpacker must learn to put aside thoughts of what the food *should* taste and look like, and appreciate the new experience in its own right! 'Freeze-dried' food is prepared by a procedure called 'vacuum sublimation'. The fresh or cooked food is 'flash-frozen'. This means it is frozen very rapidly so that the water forms tiny ice-crystals. The food is then placed in a vacuum at very low temperature, about −45.5°C (−50°F), and the ice is drawn off as water vapour. By this rather more complicated process, structural damage is avoided, so the fresh and natural flavours are not lost to the same extent as they are with air-drying.

Because freeze-drying is a sophisticated process, production costs were originally high and this meant that the process was restricted to best quality produce and the products were inevitably expensive.

Cooking on a driftwood fire during a coastal walk

However, 'assembly-line' manufacture has now been developed and freeze-dried foods are available at prices which are competitive with air-dried foods.

Whatever the process of preparation, you will find that all specialist backpacker's foods are expensive, but the costs can be kept low by supplementing the diet with dehydrated items from the supermarket shelf: nutritious soups, sauces, gravies and instant products like potato, milk, desserts, fruit juice etc. Look for convenient lightweight products and where possible reduce weight further by discarding superfluous boxes and wrappings. Make full use of polythene bags tied with wire strips (but be sure to cut out and include the panel of instructions for preparation).

The specialist backpacker's food is packed in polythene or aluminium foil coated with plastic. Such wrappings are durable and should preserve the contents in perfect condition for an indefinite period, but it is a good idea to wrap packets in extra polythene bags. Rough handling or treatment in the rucksack may cause splitting, or puncturing – even a tiny hole will allow air to enter the contents, which will then rehydrate and spoil in a short space of time.

Food requirements for energy

Food consists of a mixture of food substances, of which there are six types: carbohydrates, fats, proteins, mineral salts, vitamins and water (the latter is removed during dehydration). It is the carbohydrates and fats which provide us with our energy. Carbohydrates release their energy very soon after they are eaten, but fats have a long-term effect. They become stored in layers under the skin or round the body organs; and it is during strenuous activity or periods of prolonged physical exertion that these fat deposits are broken down to release their energy.

Units of energy made available to the body from the food we eat are called 'calories' (see p. 84). When backpacking, it is important to eat foods which are rich in carbohydrate and fat so that a good supply of calories is maintained to the body. With an insufficient supply, the body begins to weaken and tires very easily, because it does not have enough 'fuel' to keep it going. When this happens, a person may begin stumbling and find difficulty in judging times and distances. His body becomes less resistant to cold and other physical extremes, so making him a potential exposure case if conditions should deteriorate.

A good plan is to eat two main meals a day – breakfast before you move off and a good supper once you have prepared the night's shelter. During the rest of the day 'eat little and often' is the rule. As you walk, keep nibbling at high-calorie foods like nuts, raisins, cheese, chocolate, sweets, Kendal mint cake, so avoiding an 'energy gap'. (Besides, it is not advisable to stop for a big feast at midday because it is so difficult to move on again afterwards.)

Preparation

Being developed specifically for lightweight camping, dehydrated foods available in outdoor centres and camping shops are quick and easy to prepare, and require the minimum amount of fuel and equipment. The manufacturers give information on food values in special leaflets.

Alexa Products first produced their Raven Meals when they recognised the potential of dehydrated foods in lightweight camping; a pan, spoon, stove, water and ten minutes are all you need to prepare a nourishing supper. Direct Foods, under the Ranch House label, Swel Food and Springlow are other manufacturers' names to look out for.

With freeze-dried foods, this convenience can be taken one step further, in that preparing a meal now becomes simply a matter of pouring boiling water directly into the food-bag, mixing well, then leaving to stand for five minutes before eating. Such meals are available from Alexa Products' Raven Regal range, Springlow's Space Age Food range and Oregon Freeze Dry Foods under the Mountain House label.

Of course, the supermarket products are more widely available and less expensive. Pot Noodles are perhaps a layman's version of these new 'wonder' foods. Knorr produce a wide range of Quick Soups which are made with boiling water and are immediately ready for eating. The same company's Big Pack Soups (making 1½ pints) require ten minutes simmering after rehydration, but are thick, nourishing, tasty and reasonably priced. Cadbury produce several instant products including Snack Soups, Marvel (powdered milk), Smash (powdered potato) and cocoa. Kelloggs' Rise and Shine is a refreshing

Cooking supper on a 'meths' stove of integral design, one of the few that work well in a breeze

drink which only needs the addition of cold water, while hot water will make a delicious meaty drink from Oxo or Bovril. Batchelors' ready products are convenient and excellent value, including Cup-a-Soup and a variety of sauces and thick gravies.

However, do be on your guard against items which appear ideal to your needs, but may prove extravagant in terms of fuel or time. Phrases like 'simmer for thirty minutes' or 'leave to stand in a cool place overnight' are not to be overlooked. Always read directions carefully and avoid long, complicated and otherwise impractical procedures.

Supermarket items require another word of warning regarding manufacturer's directions. These cannot be taken literally. 'Simmer genty for five minutes' may be the rule for a kitchen stove, but for a primus in the open, read 'heat for fifteen minutes'. Likewise, don't be fooled by the claim 'serves two'. Two sparrows maybe, but not two ravenous backpackers. The only way to form an opinion of a product is to buy it and try it.

Enjoyable eating

It is important to enjoy your food. A good breakfast makes a fine start to the day, while after a hard day's exertions, a tasty supper makes it all seem worth while. An appetising meal can also act as a terrific

A selection of typical dehydrated foods

morale booster, or even become a life saver. So choose food that it tempting, exciting, even exotic.

Alexa Products' Raven Meals provides a choice of six main dishes – vegetable stew, rice and curry, savoury risotto, pasta and vegetable bolognese, savoury fry and scrambled egg; while their Regal Range includes shrimp curry with rice, spiced beef with potato, chicken and mushroom with rice; there are dessert dishes too – rice pudding, custard and banana, apple and strawberry. Alexa also promise the supply of many additional products in months to come.

The lightweight meals produced by Direct Foods (Ranch House products) are based on 'protoveg', a protein product prepared directly from soyabean, so containing no meat or animal fat. It is available as Natural Protoveg which you flavour with cheese, marmite, tomato sauce or whatever, according to your own tastes; or as a flavoured base in a range of meals including vegetable stew, vegetable bolognese, vegetable curry, vegetable mince, vegetable goulash, Sosmix, Savoury Mixture and Sizzleberg.

Springlow offer separately packed ingredients. There are de-hydrated vegetables – cabbage, diced carrot, green beans, peas, onion slices; also instant potato mix and freeze-dried chicken and beef; while their standard 'One-man/one pan' meals are available as vegetable stew with beef, curried rice with beef, pasta and chicken dinner, beef Italian, chicken risotto, scrambled egg and cheese, savoury omelette, and cheese and onion. Liver and onion followed by orange-flavoured yoghourt is just one tempting example from their appetising range called Space Age Foods.

Single ingredients are also obtainable from Mountain House Products, for example peas, beans, corn, potato, diced beef, blue-berries, strawberries, pineapple; while their range of complete meals includes shrimp creole, turkey Tetrazzini, beef stroganoff, beef stew, chicken and rice with onion, chili with beans, lasagne with meat sauce, sausage patties and macaroni cheese. Strawberry ice-cream, butterscotch pudding and banana cream pudding are examples of their dessert dishes.

So there is a wide choice available, but don't forget that when it is time to eat, it is too late to decide that you do not like the choice you made. It is best to be prepared for such a situation by having a bag of miscellaneous items which you can use for doctoring your food. A bland stew will leap to life after a pinch of curry powder; scrambled egg can be made delicious with a touch of tomato purée; add lemon juice to your bolognese, raisins to the rice, cinnamon to the apple flakes; and so it goes, making the dish sweeter, milder, spicier, milkier, fruitier, as your taste directs. Good breakfast foods include muesli and porridge.

One further point on choice of foods – be conscious of novelty products, such as Poppers (from Poly Nut Co. Ltd). A dual pack contains popcorn and cooking oil. The oil is in the form of a hard, solid block, with a high melting point, and is therefore very convenient for carrying in the rucksack. The corn takes only a few seconds to prepare and is guaranteed good fun.

Organising the menu
Make a list of foods you like, then go to the camping shop and, as finance and taste allow, find those products which suit you. Next, turn to other sources: the supermarket; delicatessen shops, which offer a variety of preserved goods, smoked meats, cheeses etc.; health food shops with nutritious cereal mixes, bran, fruit and nut preparations. You may even consider taking tinned or fresh food for the first day or so, if you are prepared to carry the extra weight incurred by such luxuries while you are yet fresh at the start of your venture.

However, the menu which you draw up should not only please your palate, but also your dietary needs. I have already mentioned the six food substances which comprise our food. Very often, too much time and effort is spent ensuring there is a comprehensive supply of vitamins and mineral salts – this is really *not* necessary to consider in this context, for symptoms of deficiency may begin to show after a couple of months of deprivation, but certainly not during a couple of weeks. It is far more important to think about fats, carbohydrates and proteins. I have referred to the importance of fats and carbohydrates as the suppliers of energy, but proteins are the basic 'body-building' materials for growth and repair. Continual growth and replacement goes on within the body all the time; damaged tissues need to be repaired, worn-out cells must be replaced and wounds healed over. Because proteins cannot be stored in the body, it is important to bring in a constant supply via the food, to ensure that this growth and repair work can take place.

Food firms realise that people living a vigorous and energetic life out in the open have a particular need for high levels of proteins, fats and carbohydrates, so the specialist backpacker's meals contain high proportions of these substances. Many of the foods have a higher nutritional value when reconstituted from the manufactured product than they did in their natural state.

As a rough guide you should be thinking in terms of 5,000kcals per day (see p. 84). A common fault of the novice backpacker is that he tends to eat too much, because he feels permanently hungry. But if the menu has been planned carefully, he should know that the dietary needs have been satiated, so why does he hunger for more? The reason is that in our normal feeding we take in a large bulk of food to provide the necessary dietary requirements, but when backpacking we are eating specialist food which provides the necessary carbohydrates, fats and proteins with as little bulk as possible. The reduction in volume of material passing through the gut causes the stomach to shrink and the accompanying sensations are often assumed to be hunger pangs.

Another possible outcome of the low bulk food is the problem of constipation. So ensure that your menu includes a mild laxative, like prunes, bran or treacle; or obtain a phenolphthalein preparation from the chemist before you go. And buy fruit and vegetables if you pass through a village or by a canal shop.

A plastic rechargeable toothpaste-type tube being sealed after filling

Packing

Having planned the menu and purchased the items, sort out each day's supply (i.e. breakfast, main meal and daytime snacks) into a separate polythene bag. This makes good sense with regards to packing the rucksack. It is also a good idea to prepare your food as much as possible before you leave home. For example, measure out instant coffee, sugar and dried milk into one bag, so all that needs to be done is boil the water and add the mixture. Re-usable toothpaste-type tubes are available into which you can put your favourite sandwich filling (jam, lemon curd, pâté etc.). Freezer polythene bags are much tougher than ordinary ones, and well worth the extra cost. Don't forget to take precautions over drinking water – if in any doubt use a water bottle or sterilising tablets.

8 Understanding your body

If you understand a little about how your body works then one day it may help you to survive and it will certainly make your backpacking more enjoyable. You should not become ill and suffer through ignorance.

Conditioning (fitness)

Backpacking is supposed to be fun and pleasant, not a painful grind. However, this can only be achieved if you are in reasonable condition. The early chapters on bivouacking emphasised the need to progress sensibly from something easy to more ambitious harder journeys. This cannot be stressed too much. Muscles need to be toned up gradually to cope with longer spells of activity and the extra weight of your rucksack. Your heart and lungs also have to adjust to the extra work you are asking them to do. This takes time. Normally it takes at least three weeks of regular exercise before any significant improvement can be noticed. You can test this out for yourself by counting your resting pulse rate (how many beats per minute), say first thing in the morning before you get up or after you have been sitting quietly for half an hour. At the end of three weeks' regular exercise your resting pulse rate should be lower.

Other parts of the body need to adapt to increased levels of exercise too, not least of which are the feet. They need time to get hardened up a bit. The digestive system also sometimes needs time to adjust to the increased physical activity. Extra exercise can have a dramatic effect on the bowels of previously sedentary people. However, nature soon puts this right.

If you have been inactive for some time start with short walks and build up the distance gradually. Go jogging two or three times a week. This will help tremendously if done regularly. Incidental training or conditioning can be done daily. Try to get out of breath at least once every day. Never use a lift or escalator, always use the stairs. Run up them if you can. London Underground users have an enviable number of steps available to them. Jog or run even short distances to and from the car, the shops or to see a friend. Once taking exercise becomes a habit it gets easier and easier and makes your weekend backpacking much more enjoyable. You will feel better too and maybe live longer. Ponder on the slogan 'Run for your life'.

Regular cycling to and from school or work is excellent too. You also save money and help preserve those finite fossil fuel reserves. Any form of sport which gets you out of breath is good but remember that jogging and running are things you can do any time, any place, without any equipment. So you have no excuse.

Normally it is easy for young people to get fit fairly quickly. Older people take longer. It all depends on your starting condition. Obviously very unfit people will need more determination and may find it a struggle at first. Middle-aged people should have a medical check-up if in any doubt. There is no such thing as instant fitness. It requires time and effort. If you are a bit overweight or have been smoking or drinking too much take it easy at first. Generally speaking young people have more energy but tire sooner than adults, who may be slow starting but have better endurance.

Energy expenditure – kcals per day. The example below shows a journey of 23 miles and 4000 feet of ascent uses up 7000 kcals

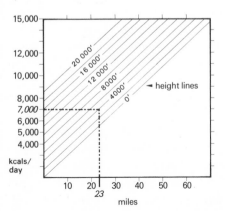

Energy requirements

'A backpacker's fuel is fluid and food'. Your body will use up about 5,000kcals in an average day's backpacking and these must be replaced (see Chapter 7). Failure to do so is folly. Not only will you slow down, become weak and maybe also suffer from excessive fatigue, nausea, dizziness and a lack of motivation to continue, but you will also become a prime candidate for 'exposure' (see pp. 97-98 on hypothermia). In any case eating and living well is all part of the enjoyment of backpacking. The worse the weather, the more strenuous the walking, the *more* you should eat, not less. You should always aim to keep yourself in good shape and not become too exhausted.

The figure of 5,000kcals per day is just an average estimate. Individual requirements vary depending on age, sex and body weight. A large person needs more calories than a small one. Ambitious journeys demand more from the body's energy reserves which need to

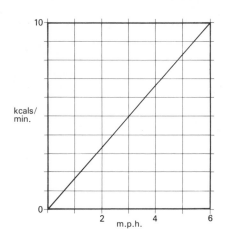

Energy expenditure while walking at different speeds on a smooth, level surface

be replaced by nourishing food. Battling through bad weather will take more out of you than a fair-weather stroll.

The diagram on the left shows the energy used when a person walks at different speeds. Walking at 2 m.p.h. uses 2.5kcals per minute, whereas walking at 4 m.p.h. used 6kcals per minute. The greater the exertion, the more energy is used. These values were measured for a subject walking on a smooth, level surface. The energy used becomes much greater when a person walks on an uneven surface, especially if there is a gradient and more so if load-carrying.

When lying down at rest a person's energy expenditure is about 1.10kcals per minute. The following table shows how energy expenditure increases with increased activity.

	kcals/min	kJ/min*	
Sits up	1.38	5.8	
Winds watch	1.60	6.7	
Stands up	1.72	7.2	*1kcal = 4.184kJ
Butters toast	2.50	10.5	1,000kJ = 1MJ (Mega
Washes windows	3.10	13.0	Joule)
Shovels coal	4.80	20.1	
Digs the garden	6.00	25.1	
Fells a tree	8.00	33.5	

In comparative terms backpacking would use energy at the rate of about 7.00kcals/min. A rough calculation of the total energy requirement for a backpacker's day is as follows:

8 hours walking at 7 kcals/min. = 7 x 60 x 8 = 3360 kcals	14.1 MJ
8 hours cooking, eating, packing, etc. at 2.5 kcals/min. = 2.5 x 60 x 8 = 1200 kcals	5.0 MJ
8 hours sleeping at 1.10 kcals/min. = 1.1 x 60 x 8 = 528 kcals	2.2 MJ
Total energy expenditure = 5088 kcals.	21.3 MJ

Dehydration

You cannot train yourself to do without water. Your body is 90 per cent fluid and normally loses 4-5 pints per day in urine, sweat and transpiration through the lungs. During exercise this normal fluid loss rises steeply due to increased sweating and breathing. In hot weather exertion it may rise to 8-10 pints per day. This must be replaced if you wish to remain healthy. Not to do so will make the body grossly inefficient due to a chemical imbalance and the usual feelings of fatigue, headache and nausea will appear. It is particularly important to drink plenty during very hot weather as dehydration makes you more susceptible to heat exhaustion – yet another dangerous condition.

Ironically, dehydration due to excessive sweating can occur in wet weather and often does, because the inadequate ventilation of water-proof clothing causes the body to become overheated. The same often applies at sub-zero temperatures due to poor clothing control, a dry atmosphere and the apparent lack of water.

Fluid losses should be replaced constantly. If urine production is significantly less than normal then you are not drinking enough liquid. Drink plenty of tea, coffee, juice or milk in the morning. Top this up at each opportunity during the day from streams or water points. In appropriate conditions carry a water bottle. Sterilise local water if in doubt with a proprietary brand of tablets. In winter cold conditions either melt snow for a midday brew, or carry a Thermos flask of hot drink. This is better than eating snow – certainly less chilling. In the evening take plenty of liquid refreshment in the form of soup and stews and finish off with copious amounts of tea or coffee. (Alcohol in any form tends to cause excessive loss of water in the urine and aggravate the condition of dehydration, not cure it.)

Remember dehyration can be cumulative and build up over a period of days. This often occurs on long trips. Do not rely entirely on nature's thirst mechanism, it does not always work. Make a conscious effort to replace the lost fluids. You can drink too little but not too much. Enjoy backpacking – keep yourself in good condition.

Body temperature regulation
'It is easier to wear a sweater than a refrigerator'. The normal body temperature is 37°C (98.4°F). Body temperatures above 41°C (106°F) and below 32°C (90°F) are incompatible with life. Human beings are essentially tropical animals striving by various means to maintain the optimum temperature which we refer to as 'normal'. At this temperature the body is at its most efficient. Temperatures two or

three degrees above or below the 'normal' usually indicate that something is wrong.

We need to burn a certain amount of fuel (food) to provide the basic energy to stay alive ('basal metabolic rate'). This process in turn produces heat. The basal metabolic rate can be increased up to tenfold to meet the energy demands of exercise or to maintain body temperature in a cold environment, often a combination of both. Whatever the circumstances heat production and heat loss must balance otherwise the body temperature will go up or down (see diagram).

Heat is lost or gained by the body in four ways:

1. *Conduction* – that is, by direct contact. For example, a person loses heat when sitting on snow or lying on cold ground and gains heat if sitting on a hot rock or radiator.
2. *Convection* – that is, by currents of air or water passing over the body as in windy conditions or running water, though it does happen most of the time by virtue of the body warming cooler air or water next to it which then rises to be replaced by more cool air or water.
3. *Radiation* – that is, by the transmission of heat rays. Obvious examples are sun rays and the heat felt from a fire. Heat is radiated from the skin to surrounding objects of lower temperature.
4. *Evaporation* – that is, by water (sweat or rain) being turned into vapour (refrigeration principle). Try for example wetting your finger and blowing on it.

Effects of heat

Heat generated in the body by strenuous exercise has to be dissipated in order to keep the body temperature normal. The body does this by allowing a lot of blood to come to the surface into the skin where some of the heat can be lost by the processes described. One of the main ways of losing lots of heat is by the evaporation of sweat from the skin. Sweat is a slightly salty liquid. If the body is to remain functioning efficiently and not suffer the effects of extreme dehydration, then the water must be replaced by drinking plenty and the salt by adding extra to the diet. Failure to do so means the eventual breakdown of the cooling process resulting in a rapid rise of body

Heat production and loss

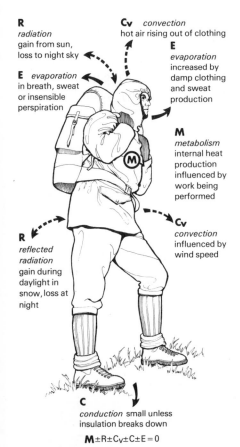

R *radiation* gain from sun, loss to night sky

Cv *convection* hot air rising out of clothing

E *evaporation* increased by damp clothing and sweat production

E *evaporation* in breath, sweat or insensible perspiration

M *metabolism* internal heat production influenced by work being performed

R *reflected radiation* gain during daylight in snow, loss at night

Cv *convection* influenced by wind speed

conduction small unless insulation breaks down

$$M \pm R \pm C_v \pm C \pm E = 0$$

temperature which can soon reach dangerous proportions and be fatal unless remedial measures are taken. (See section on First Aid for treatment of 'heat stroke' and 'heat exhaustion'.)

In hot climates, and it can happen in Britain, the heat stress can be considerable. Hot air inhibits much of the heat loss from the skin by conduction and convection. A humid climate makes it difficult to lose heat by the evaporation of sweat. In sunny conditions the body may be absorbing considerable amounts of heat by radiation from the sun and rock etc., in the surroundings, thus adding to the problem of heat dissipation. Burning of the skin (sunburn) increases the discomfort and in severe cases can cause shock, further compounding a difficult situation.

The answer is to exercise some common sense. Do not undertake strenuous exercise during the hottest part of the day until you are acclimatised. Have a siesta in the shade. Only 'mad dogs and Englishmen go out in the midday sun'. In hot sunny conditions protect yourself from direct heat absorption by covering up your body with loose, lightweight clothing. Protect especially your head and neck no matter what you look like. A broad-brimmed hat which allows ventilation is best. *Drink a vast amount of water* and include salt in your diet. Many people carry salt tablets. But be warned, these can cause vomiting if swallowed in large numbers without an adequate supply of water.

Individual tolerance to the sun's rays varies considerably. Some people's skins burn easily, others do not. Use a good filter cream if in doubt. In the hills and on snow you may need to use 'glacier cream' (a thicker, tougher paste than normal anti-sunburn preparation). The nose and lips are particularly prone to burning in these environments (see illustration facing). The eyes too will need protection, especially if there is a lot of glare from rock or snow. Polaroids and proper snow goggles are very good. Beware of cheap plastic sun glasses. They may not be effective.

Effects of cold
Man, the tropical animal, has learnt to live in cold climates by creating a micro-climate next to his skin by the use of garments, and by learning how to protect himself from the worst of the weather in a shelter of some kind.

Sunburnt noses can be very painful. Protect with a dressing tucked underneath the sunglasses or stuck lightly to the cheekbones. Protect the eyes with sunglasses and the nose and lips with 'glacier cream'

If for some reason, say bad design, insufficient planning or an accident, heat loss exceeds heat production then the inner body temperature will fall below normal. This means the person affected is in a dangerous, potentially fatal, condition and remedial action must be undertaken immediately (see Chapter 9).

In the early stages the condition is known as 'exposure', and if deep body temperature falls below 35°C it is called hypothermia. It is often

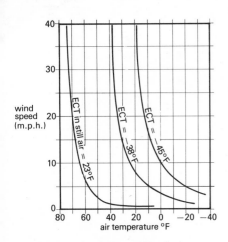

wind speed (m.p.h.)

air temperature °F

ECT in still air = 23°F
ECT = −38°F
ECT = −45°F

Wind chill chart (ECT = Effective Chilling Temperature)

	Oct.	Nov.	Dec.	Jan.	Feb.	Mar.	Apr.	May
Monthly mean °F	44	37	34	33	33	36	40	46
Mean monthly minima °F	21	20	14	12	14	17	22	27
Absolute minima °F 1869-1954	15	9	−7	−4	−14	−2	5	16

Kinder Scout/Bleaklow Hill weather statistics

associated with exhaustion (see p. 97). Most commonly it happens in British hills during wet windy conditions to people who are unfit, under-fed (therefore easily exhausted, see p. 77) or inadequately dressed. The wind transports heat rapidly away from the body. This is referred to as 'wind-chill'. The adjacent chart shows the effective chilling factor for different temperatures and wind speeds. You can see from the second chart how often temperatures fall below these levels in one hilly area. If the clothing is wet, due to rain or falling into water, and is unprotected by impervious 'shell clothing' (see p. 68), then the evaporative heat losses will be tremendous in the wind and will almost certainly outstrip the body's heat production.

Of course hypothermia can occur in snow and sub-zero temperatures and also in cold water (melt-water streams, mountain tarns and lakes), in fact in any situation where heat loss exceeds heat production. Prevention is better than cure. Prevent the onset of hypothermia by eating plenty of high energy food, by not attempting too ambitious a route in bad weather (therefore avoiding exhaustion), by wearing adequate clothing, and by retreating or bivouacking in good time whilst you still know what you are doing and have enough energy to do it.

Exposure is an insidious condition. It creeps up on you unawares. Backpacking with close friends is a good insurance policy for they will realise sooner than anyone else if a person is behaving out of character – a sure sign that the temperature of the blood going to the brain is below normal. Other signs and symptoms and advice on what to do are given in Chapter 9. The solo backpacker, with experience, can judge for himself that all is not well. Feeling very cold, shivering uncontrollably, stumbling and light-headedness (a feeling of being a little drunk) are danger signs. Intellectual reasoning (common sense) soon disappears at this stage. Hopefully, training, instinct and the will to survive will make him seek immediate shelter (tent or emergency bivouac plus sleeping bag) and a hot brew.

There is great individual variation in people's ability to withstand cold. Adolescents brought up in centrally-heated homes, schools and generally warm places are especially at risk. Case studies show a high incidence of exposure occurring after five or six hours' strenuous walking in wet windy conditions. It is a good idea to be near your next camp site or safety within this time scale in these circumstances.

9 First aid

Like most topics in this book, first aid is a very practical subject and is best learnt by attending a recognised First Aid course. It is not possible here to discuss first aid in detail, but some important points are dealt with. You should read a very good booklet called *Mountaineering First Aid* by Dick Mitchell, published by The Mountaineers, Seattle, Washington, U.S.A. (1975).

First Aid in remote areas poses different problems from many found in the urban environment though fundamentally the priorities are the same:

1. Prevent further injury
2. Maintain breathing and circulation
3. Stop bleeding
4. Treat for shock
5. Seek help
6. Evacuate

1. *Prevent further injury.* For example, remove victim from danger of further rock falls, from burning tent, from under rocks, water, snow or edge of cliff.
2. *Maintain or restore breathing and circulation.* Mouth-to-mouth resuscitation is the most effective method if breathing has stopped.
3. *Stop bleeding.* Your instinct and common sense are usually correct. Direct pressure with hand, pad (handkerchief, towel, dressing etc.) will normally succeed.
4. *Treat for shock.* Shock always occurs after a serious injury and often after relatively minor ones if associated with anxiety or the the stress of exhaustion, heat, cold, fear or pain. It is a condition caused by the failure of sufficient blood to circulate in the body, resulting in a lessening of the vital functions. Except in trivial cases *shock is unavoidable* and should be *expected.*

Signs and symptoms are pale, cold clammy skin with profuse

sweating. Pulse rate is likely to increase, tending to become weak and thready. Breathing may be shallow and rapid. The casualty may feel faint or giddy, have blurring of vision, feel sick or even vomit, be semi-conscious and may complain of thirst. He will almost certainly be very anxious or distressed. After suffering an injury solo backpackers may be able to recognise many of the symptoms in themselves and should carry out the treatment as far as possible. It is impossible to 'will' them away.

The treatment is to lay the casualty down so as to make the best use of a lessened circulatory volume. Endeavour to maintain the casualty's body temperature at normal by insulating him from the cold ground (sleeping mat) and cover him with a sleeping bag. If possible treat the injury or underlying cause of shock and place in sleeping bag if practicable. In bad weather, wet windy conditions especially, get him under cover as soon as possible whether in a tent, bivouac or 'polybag'. Unless professional medical aid is close at hand, encourage the victim to sip a hot sweet drink. Obviously this does not apply in cases where internal injuries are suspected, where vomiting is present or the victim is unconscious. In the latter circumstances place the patient in the recovery or face-down position. Reassure and comfort him. If the injury is not too serious the person is likely to recover spontaneously in time.

5. *Seek help.* If in the slightest doubt about a person's safety after injury or sickness seek help. (This applies to solo backpackers too.) Before leaving the casualty think hard on the course of action you are going to adopt. Discuss it with your friends or even the patient himself. Two heads are better than one. Do not leave in a panic. Ten minutes thinking over the best course of action, can save hours later on and may save lives. Many times have people arrived in the valley to alert the rescue teams without knowing where they have left their friends in the mountains.

Write down as much information as possible – names, nature of injury or sickness (symptoms), time, ages, equipment available and location (description and map references). The reason for this is that the person seeking help may arrive at civilisation in poor condition, maybe incoherent due to

An improvised carry using a split coiled climbing rope

hypothermia, exhaustion or dehydration. Inaccuracies of memory are all too common under stress. The written information will enable the rescue personnel to assess the situation more accurately, saving time, suffering and possible tragedy.

Also before leaving, mark the place (especially if it is a bivouac site) with a bright coloured article (red rucksack, towel, spare clothing) or an improvised flag or by stretching a long rope across the ground. Anything which will help the rescue team to find the site more easily. When all has been considered 'hasten slowly' to the valley. Make sure you get there. Dashing and breaking your neck on the way will help no one.

Those left behind will be faced with a long wait. They should when possible give the Alpine Distress Signal using whistle or torch: six long blasts or flashes – pause then repeat.

6. *Evacuation.* If the condition of the casualty is serious then evacuation is best left to competent rescue personnel (in some parts of the world there are no rescue teams).

In some cases of sprains and mild illnesses, or when time is important to the condition of the patient, say appendicitis or for reasons of weather or other factors, it may be thought wise or necessary to commence evacuation or even completely evacuate the casualty by improvised methods. There are so many variables to this kind of decision-making that only the people involved can judge the priorities and risks involved. However, it is worth knowing and practising improvised carries just in case (see photograph). Hopefully you will never need to use them.

Further first aid treatments

Fractures   There are about 206 bones in the body. If some of the small ones are broken, for example, fingers, forearm or toes etc., they do not normally threaten life. The unfortunate owner of the fracture should be treated for shock, have the affected limb immobilised by splinting or fastening comfortably to the body and taken to the nearest professional medical help. Fracture of major bone structures such as the femur (thigh bone), pelvis (hip bone) and spine can be life-threatening. In these cases the casualty must be treated for shock as outlined, the affected part must be supported with padding and bandages and help must be sought as quickly as possible.

Sprains   As far as the backpacker is concerned these are usually confined to ankles and knees. They can be very painful with severe swelling of the joint, caused by tearing or stretching of the ligaments, tendons and associated tissue. The treatment is to apply cold compresses locally (unless the patient is hypothermic) in order to reduce swelling. After an hour or two support the joint with a firmly bound crêpe or elastic bandage. Rest the limb if possible. Sometimes it is best to leave the boot on a sprained ankle until a point of safety or camp is reached. Unfasten the laces and put bandage over boot and ankle (see illustration below). The reason is that once the boot is off it may not be possible to put it on again due to the swelling.

Sprained ankle being supported by a crêpe bandage over the boot. Wet with cold water to reduce swelling unless patient is hypothermic

Strains   These are painful muscles caused by tearing or over-stretching of the muscle fibres. Rest and the application of heat to promote healing is the best treatment.

Tender blisters can be protected by
carefully fashioned foam-backed
plaster

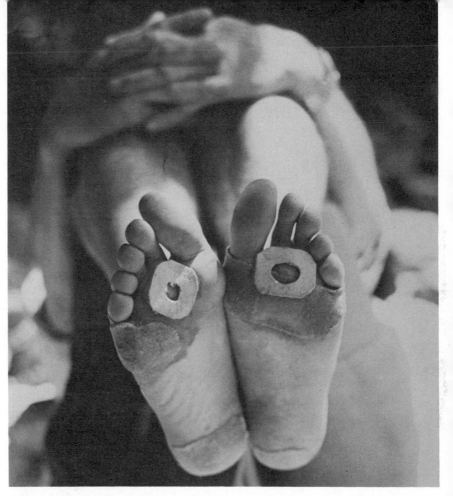

Blisters   These are mostly caused by local overheating due to friction. Deep blisters under the thick skin on the soles of the feet are caused by heat and excessive compression due to carrying a heavy rucksack. The surface-type blisters are best punctured with a sterile needle to prevent spreading, and then covered up with plaster. The skin should first be washed clean to reduce the risk of infection.

Compression blisters are not so easy to drain as they are too deep. The only other way is to protect the blisters by cutting a hole in some self-adhesive foam padding (available at most chemists) and applying it round the blister (see photograph above).

Again prevention is better than cure. At the first signs of rubbing or

95

tenderness stop and cover the area with some stretch adhesive plaster without a dressing on. In other words stick on a second layer of artificial skin.

Heat exhaustion   This is due mostly to dehydration (water loss) and leads to a shocked condition giving rise to rapid pulse, cold clammy skin, thirst, fatigue and giddiness. If untreated it can lead to delirium and coma. Urine output is low.

If similar symptoms exist coupled with muscle cramps and no marked rise in body temperature then salt deficiency is also a factor. Treat the patient by placing in a cool shady place. Restore the water and salt balance by giving him lots of cool water containing salt to drink (½ teaspoonful per pint).

Heat stroke   This is failure of the body's temperature-regulating mechanism. The onset is sudden and may be preceded by heat exhaustion. It is very serious as the body temperature is probably increasing all the time. The main symptoms are high body temperature, hot dry skin – the *absence* of sweating – maybe aggressive behaviour and lack of co-ordination. Convulsions, coma and death are likely to follow unless effective treatment is given. Obviously the patient must be cooled down by whatever means are available. For example, remove all clothing, splash tepid water over the body, generate air movement by fanning. If water is scarce lay wet cloths on the patient and create air movement over him. Heat will be lost by evaporation of the water. Make the patient rest and administer cool salt drinks (see previous paragraph).

Burns   As far as the backpacker is concerned these are usually minor except when associated with stove and fuel accidents or burning tents.

All but minor burns should be taken seriously. In all cases cool the affected part by immersion in cold water or by covering with wet cloths and irrigate. Do not burst any blisters. After a time cover the affected area to exclude the air with either dry cloths (clean handkerchiefs, underclothing) or wrap in clean polythene (bags, torn up sack liner or bivvy bag). Shock can be severe and must be treated. Seek medical help and evacuate. If the face is burned due to a cooking stove malfunction or carelessness then urgent treatment may be required as the mouth or throat may swell up and impair breathing.

Alert medical help if possible. Evacuate the victim using improvised methods if necessary. Time is not on your side.

Hypothermia (deep body cooling)

Hypothermia is often referred to as exposure and is not an uncommon complaint on British hills. The backpacker is unlikely to suffer from hypothermia unless he has been foolish. He has all the equipment to survive and protect himself provided he does not become too exhausted to use it.

Exhaustion (energy reserves burnt out) and hypothermia (body temperature below normal) go hand in hand. The backpacker is quite likely to meet young hill walkers in this condition in bad weather.

The signs and symptoms in the early stages are white or pale complexion, violent shivering, complaints of cold. Characteristically the victim loses interest in what is happening, slows down and may stop complaining of the cold. As the blood going to the brain cools further, judgement will be impaired, abnormal or irrational behaviour may be displayed, slurring of speech, disturbed vision, stumbling and falling will also occur. These are very serious symptoms. The treatment is to stop all travel and exercise. Get the person out of the wind immediately. Conserve what energy is left in the victim. Cut off all further heat loss. If shelter (e.g. a tent) and dry clothes are available remove wet clothing and place casualty into dry clothes and/or sleeping bag. Insulate by surrounding the patient with at least two inches of still air. Also supply additional warmth by placing fit, healthy (therefore warm) person(s) alongside him. Skin-to-skin contact provides the best heat transfer. Give the sufferer plenty of hot drinks and high-energy-giving food such as sugar, sweets, chocolate etc. Make sure he is well-insulated underneath, with extra sleeping mats or people. If no shelter or dry clothes are available then wrap the person in extra clothes and materials and place in two polythene bags (see diagrams on p. 98). The principles are the same: provide hot drinks and energy food as well as cutting off *all* heat loss. If this is achieved then the casualty should rewarm spontaneously in a few hours. If not then he will continue to deteriorate. Muscle rigidity, convulsions, collapse and unconsciousness are likely to occur before death.

Never underestimate the seriousness of hypothermia. Death can occur within one hour of the onset of symptoms. People's tolerance to

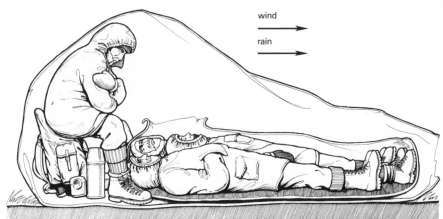

wind →

rain →

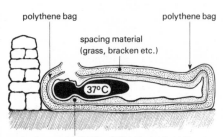

polythene bag

polythene bag

spacing material
(grass, bracken etc.)

37°C

dry, incompressible insulation (foamed polythene,
thick sweaters etc.)

Supplying additional warmth to a
hypothermia sufferer by means of
other warm bodies. Using two
polythene bags improves the
insulation (above). It is important to
keep the body core temperature at
37°C; the extremities are less
important

wind →

rain →

cold varies enormously. Whenever possible seek immediate help.
Look out for cases of incipient exposure in other members of the
group.

Note   If you chance upon someone apparently suffering from exposure and
showing no signs of life, do not presume death until a medically
qualified person confirms it. As previously described, reduce heat
loss, supply external warmth if possible and evacuate. Handle the
casualty gently as a cold but not dead patient, because the heart may
be in a delicate condition.

If no pulse can be felt do not on any account try external cardiac massage as this may cause fibrillation (or random contraction of individual muscle fibres) which could be irreversible and by itself prevent recovery. As the person's body rewarms, the heart will re-commence beating of its own accord if death has not occurred.

First aid kit (see p. 66 for suggested kit)

The backpacker's first aid kit needs only to be simple. The requirements are for something to treat everyday ailments such as sore feet, minor cuts and abrasions, sprains, indigestion, headaches etc. Anything more serious can usually be solved with knowledge, skill, improvisation and by seeking help.

'Shell' dressings are a must for the first aid kit. They are sold in a range of sizes. Here a large one is being applied to a badly grazed knee

Northumberland coastal walk

Camping in upper Eskdale in the Lake District

10 Where to backpack

Armed with the 'know-how' and experience of independent travel on foot, then a whole world is open to you. You could go backpacking in Britain almost every weekend and not do the same route twice. There are ten National Parks, many long-distance paths and over a hundred recognised walks of all grades, far too numerous to list in this book. New ones are being thought out all the time. Further information on these can be obtained from sources such as the Ramblers Association Fact Sheet (published annually), the Countryside Commission, National Park information centres, the Backpackers' Club and the Long Distance Walkers Association to mention a few (see list of useful addresses and bibliography). Local libraries and books can be a great help as well as such monthly magazines as *Climber and Rambler* and *The Great Outdoors*. The magazines usually have lists of club names and addresses, reviews of equipment and information on routes and footpaths.

However, it is often more interesting to work out your own routes. Planning them is much more fun. A lot depends on where you live and transport arrangements. With a map and some imagination all kinds of possibilities come to mind. For example, work out routes which take in places with the same word in their name such as 'fell', 'tarn', 'cairn', 'down', 'laithe', 'tor' etc., or visit as many historical sites (marked on O.S. maps) as you can. Try to see if it is possible to follow a water-shed or even a river or stream to its source. In some areas it is possible to follow the parish or county boundary or even old country boundaries such as Offa's Dyke and Hadrian's Wall. Coastal paths make popular walks; remember you can usually camp on the foreshore (Crown Land) which lies between high and low tide marks. Consult local tide tables first. Some people like to walk from coast to coast and have a swim at the start and finish. A popular one is from the North Sea to the Irish Sea.

Other ideas are to discover and follow ancient routes such as drove roads (the Lake District and Scotland), green lanes (the Yorkshire Dales) and Roman roads (all over Britain). In some areas disused railways lines are a possibility. Canal tow paths are not very hilly but they can often link other paths and routes together. They are sometimes a very good way of walking out of towns and cities into the open countryside. (Strictly speaking you need a permit from the British Waterways Board.) Woods, moors and forests offer plenty of scope. Forest trails (often waymarked) make good introductory walks as do many nature trails. In mountainous areas there is no need to follow the 'trade routes' along the ridges and summits like most people do. Try working out safe routes to visit as many lakes or tarns as possible. They make good camping sites. Alternatively, see how many summits and tarns you can visit in a journey. This kind of route takes you away from the crowds on to little-trod areas even in the more popular places. Really fit people like to take on challenging walks, covering long distances in a weekend – 100 miles is not unusual. Others set a height target such as ascending the equivalent of Mount Everest (29,028 feet) in a weekend. There is no end to the kind of things people dream up.

Every square centimetre of land in Britain belongs to someone, though thousands of miles of public rights of way do exist and are now shown in the latest 1:50,000 O.S. maps. You should be able to follow these safely and without let or hindrance. Any problems should be reported to the local authority. The laws relating to footpath access and trespass are very complex, and general advice is difficult to give. Courtesy and common sense should prevail. In the event of an accidental trespass extreme politeness and retreat will usually keep you out of trouble.

Orienteering has become very popular and provides good practice with map and compass. Some big two-day events, the Karrimor Mountain Marathon for example, are held annually and have a class suitable for backpackers who prefer to walk and camp as opposed to run and camp. On these events there are usually about 1,000 lightweight tents at the overnight camp site. If you look around you will learn a lot about lightweight gear.

Winter snow adds a new dimension to backpacking. In the hills a lot of care, skill and experience of winter mountaineering is essential. Backpacking in the valley snow is good fun and opens up lots of

Some of the tents at the Karrimor Mountain Marathon

Backpacking in the Isle of Skye

Cross-country skiing overnight camp

A challenging journey through the
mountains of Turkey

possibilities. The rudiments of cross-country skiing can easily be learnt in half a day, and travelling on skis on undulating ground is easy and less tiring than walking. Backpacking on skis is popular in Scandinavian countries as well as in Austria, Switzerland, France and even parts of Spain. It is worth considering a winter backpacking holiday in these places.

Spring and summer backpacking abroad provides infinite possibilities. Almost every country has its long-distance routes, similar to those in Britain only more spectacular. The Alps provide excellent backpacking possibilities, they are not just for climbers. Many other countries have wild and remote areas which lend themselves to exploration on foot. Backpacking trips in these areas take on the proportions of a mini-expedition. With the improvement in travel even places as far apart as Nepal and America come within reach of more and more people.

Some countries just outside Europe – Algeria, Morocco and Turkey for example – offer exciting possibilities. Special care should be taken to consult the appropriate embassies and tourist offices for information. It often takes a long time to obtain the necessary documentation so plan well ahead (one year). Also seek medical advice on inoculations and vaccination. Take some medication to combat stomach upsets which tend to affect Europeans rather badly. Very important too is to obtain as much knowledge as you can about the traditions, customs, religion and ethics of the country you propose to visit. Such things as bare arms, bare legs, men with long hair, girls in trousers, are all things which can cause offence in some communities. My experience is that most people are friendly and curious towards strangers. If the local people are hostile then there is usually a good reason though it may not seem logical to you.

Related hobbies

Backpacking is often a means to an end though for most people it is enjoyable in its own right. It enables you to travel into remote areas to see what is there and brings out something of the explorer in all of us. Photography, the study of wild flowers or animals may be the underlying motive for the journey. Birdwatching, star gazing, rock climbing, skiing and caving can all become part of backpacking.

Frequently people take to backpacking for a variety of reasons then

Backpacking and caving in Algeria

become interested in some of the topics I have mentioned. Most people like to have a camera to record parts of their journey and the things they have seen. Log books, a favourite hobby with some people, benefit greatly from a few pictures. They also impress one's friends.

Safety in remote areas

Nowadays 'risk recreation' seems to be becoming more popular than ever. Hang gliding, climbing, diving and racing fast machines are all done *voluntarily* by thousands of people. Why do they do it? A profound question for you to think about on the trail.

Generally speaking, backpacking would not come into the same category but you would be deluding yourself if you thought there was no danger or risk involved, especially if you go into remote areas. Risk cannot be removed from the business of living, even staying in bed has its dangers.

Safety means exercising common sense and sorting out a proper set of values. There is only one experience in life from which we can learn nothing – and that is dying. Taking a calculated risk (is it worth it?) is one thing, throwing one's life away through sheer stupidity is another. Be brave enough to be a coward and turn back if things look like getting out of hand. Remember the hills and mountains are not going to run away, they will still be there waiting for you as long as you live.

The further you go into remote areas the greater the risks and the rewards. If you cannot accept that, don't go. There are objective dangers such as storms, stonefalls, flash floods, avalanches, wild animals etc., over which we have no control, though experience and judgement count for a lot. The subjective dangers, that is the ones under our own control, can be reduced by good planning, preparation, equipment and experience. There is no substitute for knowledge.

This book has emphasised the need to build up experience gradually, slowly progressing from the known into the unknown, discovering yourself as you go along (known as the 'inward journey') as well as learning a great deal on the way. The definition of a good backpacker is the same as for a good mountaineer: 'someone who has been doing it for a long time and is still alive'.

There is nothing to fear going into remote areas provided you are reasonably fit, have good food, equipment, a knowledge of how your body works, are skilled with map and compass and competent on your legs (planning, preparation and knowledge). Make some emergency arrangements just in case.

Always have a healthy respect for the forces of nature – humility can be a life saver.

Journey's end

Appendix: Fibres and fabrics

'Clean Fabrics perform best'.

The purpose of this Appendix is to help backpackers have a better understanding of the very complex world of textiles, which to anyone outside the trade is a veritable jungle.

In simple terms, there are four factors to be considered:
1. The properties of the basic fibres and filaments themselves.
2. The fabric construction – that is, the way the basic fibres and/or filaments are put together.
3. The treatments or 'finishes' given to either the basic fibres or the end fabric.
4. The final construction of the garment or product – that is, the way it is cut and fixed together.

A great many variables occur under each heading creating a bewildering number of permutations. Availability of the raw materials and the cost at every level of production are additional factors influencing the final product. In the end most items are a compromise between what is technically possible and the amount of money people are prepared to pay for it.

Fibres

Before looking at some of the properties of the basic fibres it is important to appreciate that the fibres themselves fall into three main groups:
1. Natural fibres derived from (a) animals (e.g., wool), (b) plants (e.g., cotton).
2. Regenerated fibres (man-made fibres) so called because they are textile fibres constructed by man from naturally occurring sources of cellulose such as trees (viscose) or protein such as ground nuts.
3. Synthetic fibres made entirely from chemicals (e.g., nylon).

Natural fibres

In the category of animal fibres *wool* is the best known and most common textile fibre. The fleece of the Merino sheep is the main source of supply, accounting for 90 per cent of the world's wool production. For centuries man has used woollen garments to keep him warm and it is still very popular for this purpose today. The reason for this is that approximately 80 per cent by volume of a wool garment is air. Air is well known to be a poor conductor of heat and as a consequence woollen clothing is eminently suitable for use as an insulating layer in a clothing assembly. Furthermore, the moisture-absorbing properties of the wool fibre (up to 35 per cent of its own weight of water) means that it feels dry and comfortable even when very wet. One disadvantage of wool fibre is that it is covered with microscopic horny scales and in its natural state is fairly weak and extensible; it becomes more so when wet and is prone to excessive shrinkage and matting due to the tangling and interlocking action of the scales. However, modern 'superwash' treatments have largely eliminated these problems and most woollen garments can now be machine-washed.

For use in garments, the original fleece has to be scoured (washed clean), teased-out (disentangled) and drawn into a sliver of parallel fibres before being spun into a yarn. Generally speaking, the more bulky 'woollen yarns' are used for knitted-type garments such as socks, mitts and sweaters, whilst the tighter-spun, harder 'worsted yarns' are used for trousers and jackets.

Garments made of wool can be highly recommended to the backpacker. Wool has stood the test of time and whilst synthetics rival it in some areas there is simply no substitute yet for a good pair of woollen socks or a 'woolly Balaclava'.

Cotton, a natural fibre of plant origin, has been used by man to make clothing since Egyptian times.

It is grown in vast quantities in India, Egypt and the U.S.A. The fibre is found in the seed pods of the cotton plant and is put to a wide range of uses from delicate lace-making to heavy-duty ropes and canvas. Cotton is a moderately strong fibre which does not stretch easily and unlike wool actually gains strength when wet.

One property of cotton the backpacker should know about is that when cotton fibres become wet they do not recover from deformation and thus make better contact with the skin. That is why it is felt to be a 'cold' fabric. For this reason it is popular and functional in hot climates when one is trying to remain cool. Conversely, this cooling property makes cotton garments inappropriate for use in the cold, wet environment so frequently experienced on British hills. In particular cotton denim jeans, which are very popular with young people because of their hard-wearing properties and figure-hugging styles, can be lethal in wet, cold conditions. The cotton denim is made from tightly twisted yarns which entrap a smaller amount of air than most cotton yarns, so the insulation they provide is less than woollen fabrics. Also, when wet the air voids fill with water and due to the tight-fitting construction lead to a high rate of heat loss from the body by conduction through the fabric and the liquid water present. Hypothermia can quickly result. For these reasons the wearing of jeans cannot be recommended.

However, a fine, tightly-woven cotton fabric called Ventile has been used for making 'shell clothing' such as anoraks for a long time. It is windproof and turns a lot of rain yet 'breathes' (allows perspiration to pass through). It works on the principle that the tightly-woven cotton threads swell when wet, making it very difficult for the rain to pass through. One disadvantage is that it becomes rather stiff when this happens. Personally, I have never been without a Ventile anorak in the last twenty years. I find them very serviceable, hard-wearing and for practical purposes wind and waterproof. They can be laundered and the water-repellant properties can be improved by a quick spray from a silicone aerosol.

Lightweight, finely-woven cotton fabric was the traditional material for making backpackers' tents. It is still in use by some manufacturers though it has been largely superseded by nylon fabrics which are stronger, weight for weight. Cotton tent fabrics, however, unlike proofed nylon, 'breathe' and condensation within the tent is avoided.

Cotton is prone to rotting by mildew in damp atmospheres and great care should therefore be taken to store cotton fabrics in an absolutely dry condition.

Regenerated fibres

The family of regenerated fibres (man-made fibres) have little to offer the backpacker. *Viscose, Rayon, Sarille* and *Tenasco* are typical examples of natural polymers being dissolved and regenerated as fibres. On the whole they have poor abrasion resistance, are weak and even weaker when wet. *High Tenacity Viscose* has a high wet strength though this is low in comparison with cotton and nylon. Fibres made from chemically modified cellulose such as *Dicel* and *Tricel* are stronger than *Viscose* but are still relatively weak and have poor resistance to abrasion.

Generally speaking, man-made fibres on their own have similar thermal properties to cotton, are the basis of many cheap materials and on the whole cannot be recommended to the backpacker. However, sometimes they occur blended with other fibres to produce an excellent material. A good example of this is the *Super Helanca* fabric used by Rohan which is made of *Viscose, Lycra* and *Nylon* and has properties similar to traditional *Ventile.*

Synthetic fibres

Synthetic fibres and materials – that is, made entirely from chemicals – make the greatest contribution to the life of the backpacker. One of the best-known of these is nylon. It is produced in three types: low strength with high extension used for clothing; medium and high strength, both with low extension, used for ropes, tapes and webbing. Several types of nylon have been developed but the main two fibres likely to be encountered are spun from the polymers Nylon 6 (Continental) and Nylon 6.6 (U.K.). The difference between them is small, though the latter has a higher melting point (250°C). Generally speaking, nylon fibres are noted for their strength, elasticity, flexibility, resistance to abrasion, relatively low water absorption (8 per cent of moisture by weight), rot-proofness and their inertness to a wide range of chemicals – though they are not immune to acid. Careless storage of safety equipment such as climbing ropes and harnesses in close proximity to acid batteries could lead to disastrous results in the event of a leakage.

These wide-ranging properties make nylon eminently suitable for use in 'shell clothing', tents, sleeping bag fabrics, rucksacks, gaiters, straps, laces and ropes.

Another common group of synthetics are the polyesters which have trade names such as *Terylene* and *Dacron*. Polyesters have similar characteristics to nylon but differ mainly in their elongation properties, stretching only a short distance before breaking. This relative lack of elasticity makes polyester ropes more suitable than nylon for caving, harness webbing and as fixed ropes in mountaineering. Polyester fibres absorb very little water, are non-allergic and extremely resilient. They are widely used in all types of clothing manufacture and as filling for duvets and sleeping bags, when they are known by such names as *Fibrefil, Hollofil* and *P3*. Sleeping bags and other articles made of polyester are easy to wash and dry. High strength and high modulus are

useful characteristics in a sewing thread and polyester yarns are widely used in this application.

Acrylic fibres (e.g. *Acrilan* and *Courtelle*) are not as strong as nylon but have large amounts of stretch and a high elastic recovery. Water absorption is very low which means that the fabric once spun to remove water from between the yarns will dry very quickly. Acrylics are mainly used in staple fibre form and find their way into circular sliver-knit fabrics as used for pile clothing (see p. 67).

A synthetic fibre which until recently had only limited success in the textile trade is *PVC*. Now, however, it has widespread use in under-garments to combat the cold known as 'thermal underwear'; amongst the best-known examples are those made by Damart Thermawear and North Cape. This type of underwear worn next to the skin can be highly recommended for use in cold environments not only by backpackers but by other outdoor enthusiasts and by the aged. It has been discovered that unlike most fibres which generate a positive electrical charge on rubbing against the skin, PVC fibres generate a negative charge. It is claimed, though not yet proven, that this negative charge of static electricity has therapeutic effects and is of value in the treatment of rheumatism and similar complaints. One disadvantage of PVC fibres is that they have a low tolerance to heat and will shrink badly if washed in over-hot water. Handwashing in

lukewarm water is best. The fibres themselves absorb little or no water and so dry easily. They do not burn and have a high resistance to many chemicals.

Finally, *Polypropylene* makes low strength, low density fibres with almost zero water absorption and is used for the same types of fabrics and garments as PVC. It can be highly recommended for sportsmen and outdoor enthusiasts alike. During strenuous exercise it appears to 'wick away' the sweat leaving the skin dry and warm. *Lifa* underwear marketed by Helly Henson of Norway is probably the best example. I have used it a lot myself in the winter months.

Fabric construction
Fabric construction is just as important as, if not more so than, the basic fibre in determining the final properties of the material. Quite simply, the textile fibres are twisted (spun) into yarns and these are then either woven on a loom or are knitted. These basic cloths can where appropriate be bonded, laminated or quilted.

Woven fabrics are made by interlacing two sets of yarns at right angles. The warp yarns run lengthwise and the weft yarns crosswise, passing under and over the warp yarns alternately. It will be realised that this relatively simple process has an infinite number of variables. For example, in a 'plain weave' where the warp and weft threads are of equal size and number, the final fabric would vary depending on the properties of the basic fibre used, the size of the threads and how tightly they were woven together. Ventile is a good example of fine cotton threads being tightly woven together to produce a cloth with characteristics useful to the backpacker.

If in a plain weave a thicker yarn is introduced, say every 6mm, then the resultant cloth will have a checked or squared pattern on it. This technique produces the well-known 'rip-stop' nylon fabrics which are widely used for making tents, sleeping bags and outer clothing because they are more resistant to tearing than a plain weave. A taffeta or ribbed appearance can be created by using a heavier weft than warp and so on. Add to this the variables of the basic fibres and possible mixtures and you will begin to appreciate the complexity of textile manufacture.

The one property which immediately distinguishes a *knitted fabric* from a woven fabric is its ability to stretch. Irrespective of the nature of the fibre type used, the loops of yarn within the fabric straighten out under tension, giving the material its characteristic elasticity. This is an important quality in that 'sizing' of the garments is not as critical as it would be with a woven cloth because the fabric tends to 'hug' the body. Also knees and elbows in the finished garment are more resistant to bursting from the bending forces applied to them.

Bulky-knit fabrics provide excellent insulation in still air due to the large amount of air trapped in the knitted loops. However, this open structure means that they give only poor insulation in winds, unlike their tightly woven counterparts which can provide a high degree of wind resistance. The prime use of knitted garments is to form the insulating layer under the wind and waterproof 'outer shell'. Damart, North Cape and Lifa garments are excellent examples of the matching of fibres to a construction to achieve a good end product. Wool of course falls into this category.

Loop-stitched socks, 'terry' and 'bouclé' effects are special knits which can be useful to the backpacker. Sliver knit is perhaps the most important special knit of interest to the outdoor enthusiast as it produces the now well-known and popular *pile fabrics*. The pile is created by passing slivers of staple yarn through the fabric loops during the knitting process. Pile fabrics are now widely used in clothing assemblies and sleeping bags. They provide a high degree of insulation in relation to weight and have the remarkable property of maintaining much of this insulation even when wet. They are in no way windproof and perform best in conjunction with a windproof and/or waterproof covering.

Field and laboratory tests have shown that sleeping bags made of sliver knit pile fabrics out-perform other more traditional types of sleeping bag in conditions of high humidity and wetness. The 'Eskimo' pile fabric mummy-shaped sleeping bag saved the lives of two potholers suffering acute hypothermia when trapped by flood waters in a deep Pyrenean cave. It not only arrested the cooling process but enabled the two men to rewarm spontaneously in a few hours, permitting them to return to the surface. No other type of sleeping bag could have achieved this in the prevailing conditions. Most pile fabrics seem to have the ability to transfer water somehow along the pile into the backing material, giving the wearer an amazing degree of comfort and protection. This material is thought by many to have superseded the traditional woollen sweater and the duvet. It is easy to wash and can be highly recommended to the backpacker for a wide range of uses. The topic of fibre pile, its properties and uses is a complex one and the reader may wish to refer to a series of articles by J. H. Keighley *et al.* in the *Clothing Research Journal* (1980), 'A Comparison of the Properties and Performance in Use of a Number of Mountain Rescue Bags', vol. 8, nos. 1 and 2.

Quilted fabrics are made by stitching together two or more fabrics with a layer of insulating material between them. The 'duvet' (French for 'down') is a well-known example using down as the insulator. Other cheaper types use Kapok padding, foam and a variety of fibre webs. Most sleeping bags to date have this construction (see p.53).

On the whole quilted fabrics have many drawbacks and cannot be recommended to the backpacker. Better alternatives are usually available.

Finally, *bonded* and *laminated fabrics* must be mentioned as these represent some of the latest developments in textile technology. These are multi-component fabrics, that is layers of different material stuck together in a sort of sandwich construction. The most important of these to the backpacker is the much-heralded and controversial 'wonder fabric' known as Gore-Tex, which is fully discussed later.

Finishes
The third major variable in textile manufacture concerns the treatment or finish given to the fibres or fabrics. The backpacker need only be concerned with those processes which are aimed at making existing fabrics such as nylon windproof and waterproof. Silicones are frequently used to make fabrics water-repellent, but in order to achieve impermeability a coating of polymers needs to be applied. There are three main types: *Polyurethane, PVC* and *Neoprene*.

Polyurethane-coated nylon is probably the most common, being widely used in the making of anoraks, cagoules, over-trousers, tents, rucksacks and gaiters. Items are marketed as having been treated with one or more layers of polyurethane. The bond is not good and it delaminates easily especially at the points of wear – under rucksack straps, at elbows and knees.

This type of proofing cannot in all honesty be recommended for use as the impervious 'outer shell' in a clothing assembly.

PVC coatings are often yellow and are widely used for sailing and motor-cycling clothing, where they have replaced the traditional 'oilskins'. They make a good bond and are impervious to wind and water. However, the disadvantage of this type of coating is that it is rather stiff when cold and can crack at low temperatures. Neoprene coatings are by far the best, having good wear and bonding properties without the disadvantages of PVC.

All coated fabrics produce condensation during wear because water vapour cannot pass through them. The innovative Gore-Tex fabric previously mentioned attempts to overcome this problem. The following extract from an article entitled 'An Assessment of the Functional and Design Requirements of Clothing used to Protect the Human Body I' by J. H. Keighley and G. Steele (*Clothing Research Journal,* vol. 8, no. 1, 1980, p. 36) should be of interest.

'The most novel fabric to be introduced on to the market during recent years has been that of Gore-Tex. This fabric is a laminate with an outer front surface of woven nylon, a second layer of Polytetrafluoroethylene (P.T.F.E.) and in some cases a knitted nylon backing fabric. The active P.T.F.E. layer of the composite appears as shown in the photograph [not reproduced here] and the

manufacturer's claim of 9×10^9 (9 thousand million) holes per square inch is substantiated by the micrograph [not reproduced here] shown. This fabric has a very low air permeability (i.e. windproof), is not permeable to liquid water (rainproof) but allows water vapour to diffuse through the material and thus should not be liable to condensation problems.

Gore-Tex is a fabric which has been the subject of much development work during the last few years and while the original fabrics were of plain weave structure using continuous filament type yarns, new yarns and hence new fabrics have been introduced with a variety of surface finishes. Early fabrics acted as 'ventile' materials but were subject to the limitation that the working P.T.F.E. layer must be kept clean. The claim that the holes in the P.T.F.E. allowed 'water vapour molecules to pass through but not liquid water' would not pass the scrutiny of the least observant scientist and this factor was hardly supported by the transmission of water when dirty. However, the manufacturers now claim that this problem has been solved.

The micrographs [not reproduced here] show the active P.T.F.E. layer and the construction of a polycotton-P.T.F.E. laminate of Gore-Tex.

All fabrics which act as barriers to liquid water have the drawback that holes are introduced when the fabric is sewn into a garment. Cotton ventile type fabrics suffer least from this problem but for all fabrics which utilise a layer of polymer, the stitch holes allow water to pass through.

The problem can be reduced somewhat by the use of a sewing thread which swells on wetting, thus tending to close up the needle hole but the success of this is very limited. Most manufacturers are obliged therefore to resort to the device of either doping the seams after the garment has been constructed or of taping the seams or both. Such processes are time consuming and expensive but essential. In order to reduce this problem, garment design must be considered in order to reduce the length of stitching to be treated and to position the seams so that they are protected from incident water.

Bonding of seams has also been attempted but this leads to a stiffening of the structure, as does taping, and is also a tedious process. Welding, however, has also been found to be useful but the flexing properties of the welded section are different from those of the fabric and can easily crack in wear. Some manufacturers have also used welding techniques for Gore-Tex fabrics but this is not a particularly satisfactory technique since the P.T.F.E. component will not melt and the welding takes places between nylon layers only. Since the strength of the P.T.F.E.-nylon laminate bond is not particularly high, the welded seam is not a strong component of the garment and this is limited to the non-load bearing areas of the garment.

The prevention of condensation inside a 'waterproof' garment is a factor which has led to considerable research and development effort over the years. However, it is clear that under certain conditions it is impossible to prevent condensation taking place. In addition, fabrics which are designed to allow water vapour to pass through the structure cannot act as a 'Maxwell's demon' for each molecule and the vapour can diffuse through in either direction. It is always assumed, however, that water vapour will pass from the inside of the garment to the outside; this is an assumption which is not always the case. Water vapour will pass through a barrier only when there is a vapour pressure gradient which acts as a driving force for this function. When the relative humidity of the atmosphere is 100 per cent, i.e. the air is saturated and it is probably either misty or raining, then it is unlikely that water will migrate from the inside of the garment (unless some other mechanism is functioning). Under these conditions, the condensation of water vapour inside a garment cannot be prevented since the relative humidity (R.H.) inside must be equal to or less than the R.H. outside. If the inside R.H. is less than 100 per cent, then diffusion of water vapour *from* the outside *to* the inside can take place. Such a problem has been found for a Gore-Tex sleeping bag cover used for a bivouac in dense mist on the hills.

Condensation will only occur when warm moist air is cooled and thus becomes saturated. When a garment is being worn under cool outdoor conditions, a temperature gradient will exist between the skin (temperature approximately 35°C) and the outside air. Thus a range of temperatures exists throughout the multiple layers of clothing present. For given R.H. inside the clothing assembly, water vapour will diffuse outwards and it is inevitable under certain conditions that at a given point in the thermal assembly, the Dew Point will be reached and hence condensation will occur. In clothing, therefore, the location of this Dew Point region will depend on the nature, constitution and thickness of the total assembly. For a thick assembly therefore, such a region may exist well within the assembly, so that it can be concluded that in order to prevent condensation, the conditions associated with the Dew Point must not be reached within the clothing structure. When many layers of clothing are used therefore, condensation is more likely to occur within the garment than when only a small number of layers are utilised.

These conditions can be reproduced in extremely cold environments when the formation of hoar frost can be induced at various points throughout the clothing structure, the location being dependent on the amount and type of clothing being worn.

This analysis can be used to explain why so many conflicting reports are recorded concerning the efficiency of the various types of clothing used to prevent condensation. Clearly, the presence or absence of condensation is dependent on such factors as the temperature and R.H. of the outside air, the rate of loss of water from the body, the amount and type of clothing worn under the garment and so on. Each case must be analysed separately. When viewed in the light of the above discussion, the behaviour of the garment becomes perfectly clear.'

Useful addresses

Backpackers' Club, 20 St Michaels Road, Tilehurst, Reading, Berks. RG3 4RP

British Mountaineering Club, Crawford House, Precinct Centre, Booth St East, Manchester M13 9RZ

British Orienteering Federation, Lea Green Sports Centre, Matlock, Derbys. DE4 5GJ

British Tourist Authority, 64 St James, London SW1

Countryside Commission, John Dower House, Crescent Place, Cheltenham, Glos. GL50 3RA

Countryside Commission (Scotland), Battleby, Redgorton, Perth

Friends of the Earth, 529 Commercial St, San Francisco, Cal. 94111, U.S.A.

Long Distance Walkers Association: Alan Blatchford, 11 Thorn Bank, Onslow Village, Guildford, Surrey GU2 5PL

Ordnance Survey, Romsey Road, Maybush, Southampton SO9 4DH

Ramblers Association, 1-4 Crawford Mews, York St, London W1H 1PT

Youth Hostels Association, Trevelyan House, 8 St Stephen's Hill, St Albans, Herts.

D.I.Y. material suppliers Kit Line, P.O. Box 3, Stroud, Glos. GL5 5HQ

Pennine Boats, Hard Knott, Holmbridge, Huddersfield, W. Yorks. (extensive range of materials, not just for boats)

Tor Outdoor Pursuits, 5 Lyndon Grove, Runcorn WA7 5PP

For suppliers of food, equipment etc., consult the current outdoor magazines.

Bibliography

The following list is by no means complete.

General   Anderson, S., *Baron Von Mabel's Backpacking* (Rip Off Press/ Cordee, 1980).

Blackshaw, Alan, *Mountaineering: from Hill-Walking to Alpine Climbing* (Penguin Books, 1970).

Booth, Derrick, *The Backpacker's Handbook* (Charles Letts, 1972).

Booth, Derrick (ed.), *Backpacking in Britain* (Oxford Illustrated Press, 1974). Excellent photographs by Robin Adshead.

Burton, Robert, *Exploring Hills and Moors* (EP Publishing, 1976).

Carra, Andrew J., *The Complete Guide to Hiking and Backpacking* (Winchester Press, 1977).

Cranfield, Ingrid and Harrington, Richard, *Off the Beaten Track* (Wexas Travel Handbook, Wexas International Ltd, 1977). Contains a number of useful addresses, especially for the backpacker abroad.

Greenbank, Anthony, *Walking, Hiking and Backpacking* (Constable, 1977).

Henley, Martin, *EP Sport Orienteering* (EP Publishing, 1976).

Langmuir, Eric, *Mountain Leadership* (Scottish Sports Council, 1973).

Leathart, Scott, *Exploring Woodlands and Forests* (EP Publishing, 1978).

Livesey, Peter, *EP Sport Rock Climbing* (EP Publishing, 1978).

Lumley, Peter, *Backpacking* (Teach Yourself Books, English Universities Press, 1974).

Manning, Harvey, *Backpacking: One Step at a Time* (Vintage Books, 1975).

Rambling and Youth Hostelling (Know the Game Series, EP Publishing, 1976).

Spencer, Kate and Lumley, Peter (eds.), *The Backpackers' Guide* (Kate Spencer Agency: annual editions).

Styles, Showell, *Backpacking: a Comprehensive Guide* (Macmillan, 1976).

Van Lear, Denise, *The Best About Backpacking* (Sierra Club, 1974).

Waterman, L. and G., *Backwoods Ethics* (Stone Wall Press, 1977).

Westacott, Hugh, *Walkers' Handbook* (Penguin, 1980).

Whitlock, Ralph, *Exploring Rivers, Lakes and Canals* (EP Publishing, 1976).

Weather   Forsdyke, A. G., *The Weather Guide* (Hamlyn, 1969). An excellent introductory guide.

The Meteorological Office, *A Course in Elementary Meteorology* (H.M.S.O., 1962). Very good, but quite advanced despite the title.

Unwin, Daniel J., *Mountain Weather for Climbers* (Cordee, 1978 249 Knighton Rd, Leicester).

Watts, Alan, *Instant Weather Forecasting* (Adlard Coles, 1968).

Weather (Know the Game Series, EP Publishing, 1976).

First aid   Mitchell, Dick, *Mountaineering First Aid* (The Mountaineers, 1975). Very good and pocket-sized.

Renouf, Jane and Hulse, Stewart, *First Aid for Hill Walkers and Climbers* (Penguin Books, 1978).

St John Ambulance Association, *First Aid* (1980).

Ward, Michael, *Mountain Medicine* (Crosby Lockwood Staples, 1975).

Map reading   Cliff, Peter, *Mountain Navigation.* (Available direct from P. Cliff, Ardenbeg, Grant Rd, Grantown-on-Spey, Moray, 1980)

Where to backpack   Berry, G., *Across Northern Hills* (*Westmorland Gazette,* Kendal, 1975). Contains a detailed description of ten long-distance walks.

Bezruchka, S., *Trekking in Nepal* (Cordee, 1981).

Duerden, F., *Rambling Complete* (Kaye & Ward, 1978).

Millar, T. G., *Long Distance Paths* (David & Charles, 1977).

A list in this section would be endless; write off for the Ramblers Association Fact Sheet, which is published annually (see list of useful addresses). Also contact Cordee, Freepost, Leicester, who stock trail guides to most parts of the world.

Smith, R., *The Winding Trail* (Diadem, 1981).
Spring, I., *100 Hikes in the Alps* (Edwards/Cordee, 1979).
Wilson, K. and Gilbert, R., *The Big Walks* (Cordee, 1980).
Wainwright, A., *A Coast-to-Coast Walk* (*Westmorland Gazette,* Kendal, 1973).

Magazines *Climber and Rambler* (monthly).
The Great Outdoors (monthly).